"Dr. John Pilch's *Stephen* is not a 'deacon —ancient or modern— rather a Mediterranean collectivist, a Greek-speaking Hellenist-Judean honored by provoking his antagonists to violence, a minister who cares for the neglected widows among his people, and a holy man who experiences altered states of consciousness. Pilch's cultural-anthropological portrait is new and distinctive. It will tease the imagination and challenge readers to re-think the one whose terrible death changed the life of the Apostle Paul forever."

—*Dennic C. Duling, PhD*
Canisius College
Buffalo, New York

"This book is an engaging and lucid introduction to the figure of Stephen as he is portrayed in the Acts of the Apostles. A pioneer in the development of cultural anthropological approaches to the New Testament, John Pilch places Stephen the Hellenist within the context of ancient Mediterranean collectivist society. Pilch brings his particular expertise in the study of alternate states of consciousness to bear on Stephen and his companions as holy persons who have contact with the spirit realm. Readers will come away from the book with an understanding of Stephen more grounded within his particular age and culture than many other treatments of this figure."

—*Alicia Batten*
Associate Professor of Religion
Pacific Lutheran University

"John Pilch's discussion of Stephen is by no means just another book on him. Like a householder who brings forth old and new from his store, Pilch both presents old Christian materials about Stephen and offers new cultural perspectives to interpret Luke's narrative. The result is an informed, enlightened, and innovative treatment of Stephen. Like all of Pilch's writings, this book is an accessible study, a rewarding read, and an inventive exploration. The cultural lenses for interpretation have been clearly and carefully handled. 'Rich' and 'rewarding' best describe this book."

—*Jerome Neyrey, SJ*
Department of Theology
University of Notre Dame

"*Stephen* is a provocative look at the character in the Acts of the Apostles which integrates historical, grammatical, and social scientific sources to give us a fresh look at the Hellenistic martyr, which informs, corrects, and challenges the 'popular' and 'received' views. This is mandatory reading for those who wish to move beyond anachronistic and ethnocentric readings of the texts and contexts concerning Stephen."

—*Bishop F. Josephus Johnson, II*
Presiding Bishop of the Beth-El Fellowship
of Visionary Churches
Senior Pastor of The House of the Lord
Akron, Ohio

Paul's Social Network: Brothers and Sisters in Faith

Bruce J. Malina, Series Editor

Stephen

Paul and the Hellenist Israelites

John J. Pilch

A Michael Glazier Book

LITURGICAL PRESS

Collegeville, Minnesota

www.litpress.org

A Michael Glazier Book Published by Liturgical Press

Cover design by Ann Blattner. *Saint Paul,* fresco fragment, Roma, 13th century.

1   2   3   4   5   6   7   8   9

Pilch, John J.
    Stephen : Paul and the Hellenist Israelites / John J. Pilch.
       p. cm. — (Paul's social network: brothers and sisters in faith)
    "A Michael Glazier book."
    Includes bibliographical references and indexes.
    ISBN 978-0-8146-5229-9
    1. Stephen, Saint, d. ca. 36.   2. Christian martyrs—Palestine—
Biography.   3. Christian saints—Palestine—Biography.   I. Title.
    BS2520.S8P55 2008
    226.6'092—dc22
    [B]   2007041522

CONTENTS

Preface   vii

Introduction
Who Is Stephen?   ix

Chapter 1
Stephen, a Hellenist   1

Chapter 2
Stephen, a Collectivist   17

Chapter 3
Stephen, a Minister (not a Deacon!)   36

Chapter 4
Stephen, a Holy Man and His Vision(s)   51

Conclusion   67

Notes   71

Bibliography   76

Index of Persons and Subjects   80

Scripture Index   83

PREFACE

Human beings are embedded in a set of social relations. A social network is one way of conceiving that set of social relations in terms of a number of persons connected to one another by varying degrees of relatedness. In the early Jesus group documents featuring Paul and coworkers, it takes little effort to envision the apostle's collection of friends and friends of friends that is the Pauline network.

This set of brief books consists of a description of some of the significant persons who constituted the Pauline network. For Christians of the Western tradition, these persons are significant ancestors in faith. While each of them is worth knowing by themselves, it is largely because of their standing within that web of social relations woven about and around Paul that they are of lasting interest. Through this series we hope to come to know those persons in ways befitting their first-century Mediterranean culture.

Bruce J. Malina
Creighton University
Series Editor

INTRODUCTION

Who Is Stephen?

This is not as easy a question to answer as might first appear. Epiphanius of Salamis (d. 403; *Haeres.* xx.4) identified him as one of the seventy disciples chosen by Jesus (Luke 10:1), but this is entirely unreliable. He is mentioned only three times in the New Testament, all in the Acts of the Apostles. Two chapters present essentially all we know about him (Acts 6:1–8:3). He was a Hellenist, a key figure in a group of seven Hellenists. In general, Hellenists were Israelites enculturated in Greek values, language, and customs. Paul called such Israelite Hellenists "Greeks" (for example: Rom 3:9; 1 Cor 1:22-24). Most lived outside of Israel, but some returned to live there. The entire country and even Jerusalem in this period was under unavoidable Hellenist influence. Some Hellenists in Jerusalem were offended by Stephen's preaching. They persuaded others to testify falsely against him and his message. They managed to get him arrested and presented to the Sanhedrin for judgment. Here Stephen pleaded his case eloquently, but those who heard him were enraged by his speech and murdered him in a fit of establishment violence. Paul was an approving witness to the murder. Though it is difficult to date Stephen's death, the Western

Church celebrates it on December 26th. The reasoning behind this date is that since the commemoration of Jesus' birth on earth was assigned to December 25th, it is only fitting that the birth of Stephen in heaven as the first believer/martyr should be celebrated on the day after Jesus' birth.

Apart from this longer account there are two other brief references to Stephen in Acts. One reports that some fellow Hellenists who had to flee Jerusalem after Stephen's death traveled as far as Phoenicia and Cyprus and Antioch (Syria), proclaiming the gospel only to fellow Judeans there (Acts 11:19). These Judean audiences (the opposite of Greek Israelites) were quite likely very minimally acculturated to Hellenism, if at all. In other words, they did their best to avoid "contamination" by Hellenism and strove to remain "pure" in their observance of Judean traditions. They may even have continued to use the Aramaic language, at least in their own meeting houses (synagogues). Other Hellenists from Cyprus and Cyrene (North Africa) proclaimed the word to fellow Hellenists as well as to Judeans (Acts 11:19) about the Lord Jesus. Their preaching was quite successful. Many people in these Greek and Judean audiences believed! When word of this success reached Jerusalem, the community through its leaders sent Barnabas to Antioch to encourage and strengthen the faith of these new believers. He also succeeded in bringing still others into the fold. Barnabas traveled further to Tarsus to find Paul (now a believer in Jesus Messiah) and brought him to Antioch where both taught large numbers of people. Obviously by this time Paul had exchanged his conservative Judean orientation for the Hellenist approach to the Israelite tradition. Hellenists thus were the first ones to proclaim to Israelite Greeks and Judeans with a good measure of success.

The second mention of Stephen in Acts occurs in a speech crafted by Luke for Paul as he defended himself in Jerusalem before a mob stirred to anger by Paul's opponents. In this speech, Paul recounts to the mob an ASC experience that he had while praying in the temple (Acts 22:17). In the trance, the Lord Jesus advises Paul to flee Jerusalem quickly "because they will not accept your testimony about me." Jesus warns Paul that his Hellenistic understanding of the Israelite tradition and Jesus' divinely appointed place in it will not be welcomed by Judeans in Jerusalem. Paul's response to the Lord includes this statement: "And when the blood of Stephen thy witness was shed, I also was standing by and approving . . ." (Acts 22:20). Jesus replies: "Depart; for I will send you far away to the Gentiles [non-Israelites]" (Acts 22:21).[1] This reference to Paul's role in Stephen's murder testifies to the dramatic change in understanding and viewpoint that Paul underwent after Stephen's death. Because of this change, Paul is aware that he will be less successful among fellow Judeans. They no longer trust Paul nor will they accept his new perspective when they remember full well his earlier zeal for the "untainted" Israelite tradition. For this reason, the risen Jesus sends Paul to Hellenists, fellow Israelites fully acculturated to Hellenistic culture.

The Nature of Acts of the Apostles

Given this amount of information, why is the question: "Who is Stephen?" not easy to answer? The reason has to do in part with the reliability of Luke. Scholars insist that Acts of the Apostles should be classified as a historical monograph, or hagiographical history, or kerygmatic history.[2] History should remain as part of the description of this work. This is a fair request provided the modern reader realizes that the sharp distinction between fact and fiction we expect from history does not reach further back than the eighteenth century. Ancient historians such as Luke blurred that distinction. Their histories are interpreted reports rather than purely factual reports. For example, scholars recognize that the portrait of Paul presented by Luke in Acts is significantly different from the self-presentation of Paul in his authentic letters. As the Stegemanns have concluded: "In our view, the Lukan picture of Paul [in Acts] represents a literary fiction, and for the estimation of the social position of the historical Paul, his own letters have priority. The historical Paul was a citizen of neither Rome nor Tarsus."[3] Can something similar be said concerning Luke's report about Stephen: is it nothing more than another Lukan literary fiction?

In an address to a general audience on January 10, 2007, Benedict XVI demonstrated a similar critical and scholarly based reading of the information about Stephen in Acts.[4] He notes that Stephen is the most representative of a group of seven companions, but he insists that these are not "deacons"—a word that never occurs in Acts! The office and function of "deacons" is a later historical development. Thus Pope Benedict's preference for the word "companions" to describe this group is culturally appropriate for a group of collectivistic persons in a collectivistic culture, a concept which we shall explain later in this book.

Benedict XVI also recognizes that the early believers in Jesus who lived in Jerusalem were comprised of two groups: Judeans (in Latin: "Hebrews"), from the land of Israel and "others of the Old Testament Jewish faith . . . from the Greek-speaking Diaspora" known as "Hellenists." This latter is the group to which Stephen and his companions belonged. Pope Benedict continued by noting that besides tending to charitable services, Stephen also evangelized his compatriots, the Hellenists. In Jesus' name, he presented a new interpretation of Moses and of God's law. He also declared that the cult of the temple was over. Thus the speech Stephen delivered in his defense reiterated what he had been sharing with any Israelite interested in learning more about Jesus even before he was hauled before the Sanhedrin.

Though he does not use the word, Benedict XVI describes the behavior typical of collectivistic persons such as were the ancient Israelites.[5] Collectivistic persons hold the group in higher esteem than the individual. The group and its survival are paramount for a collectivistic person. Thus "charitable services" to others in their ingroup are a much higher priority for persons in collectivistic societies than for persons in individualistic societies. Individualists prefer to relegate such charitable services to organizations dedicated to these activities, though they themselves may (or may not) contribute to the support of these organizations.

Benedict XVI concluded his remarks noting that Stephen's interpretation of Moses, God's law, and the temple cult "in Jesus' name" was viewed as blasphemy by his largely Judean audience. Stephen was stoned to death for his alleged blasphemy. The Pope then exhorted his contemporary audience to imitate Stephen's virtues.

Stephen's Death

A legend reports that when Stephen was led outside the city, the appropriate place for capital punishment, Mary the mother of Jesus followed at a distance. She stood on a nearby hill with John, to whose care Jesus had entrusted her. They both witnessed Stephen's death and observed how Paul looked after the cloaks of the executioners. Both were appalled that Paul showed no pity for an Israelite facing such a violent death. Mary prayed to God to strengthen this first martyr and to receive his soul. This legend, of course, derives from a time long after Stephen was martyred. Yet as we read such legends, it is well to remember a comment by the Dominican archaeologist, Father Jerome Murphy-O'Connor about "Gordon's Tomb," mistakenly but intentionally identified as the burial place of Jesus despite a total lack of evidence to support this claim: "in Jerusalem the prudence of reason has little chance against the certitude of piety."[6] It is fair to say that piety is the driving force behind legends such as this one about Stephen, which should be interpreted accordingly. Scholars consider this legend entirely unreliable.

As for stoning, the process is described in the Mishnah. This might not necessarily have been the process to which Stephen was subjected, since Mishnaic traditions were edited by Prince Judah in Palestine around AD 200. This text, however, gives some idea of how the process was executed in that period:

> The place of stoning was twice the height of a man. One of the witnesses knocked him down on his loins. If he turned over on his heart the witness turned him over again on his loins. If he straightway died that sufficed; but if not, the

> second [witness] took the stone and dropped it on his heart.
> If he straightway died, that sufficed; but if not, he was
> stoned by all Israel, for it is written, "The hand of the wit-
> nesses shall be first upon him to put him to death and
> afterward the hand of all the people" (Deut 17:7). All that
> have been stoned must be hanged. So R. Eliezer. But the
> Sages say: None is hanged save the blasphemer and the
> idolater. (*M. Sanhedrin* 6.4)

Obviously, Stephen the alleged blasphemer was not left to
"hang out and dry" after his death. Luke concluded his report
by noting: "Devout men buried Stephen, and made great lam-
entation over him" (Acts 8:2). Burial was important in order to
preserve the body from mutilation, which in the Pharisaic belief
system would hinder resurrection. Stephen received a proper
burial. Yet Luke makes no mention of where in Jerusalem Stephen was killed or buried. Some traditions have identified St.
Stephen's Gate in the Third Wall as the place of his death, but
that is not very likely. Others have identified a place north of
Damascus gate, which is more plausible, but certitude is still
elusive.

As for Stephen's burial place, another legend fills in the gaps.[7]
In AD 415, on a Friday, a priest named Lucian who lived in
Caphargamala (about twenty miles from Jerusalem) had a dream
in which an old man richly bedecked told him to alert Bishop
John of Jerusalem that some bodies were buried in an unfitting
place. He should rebury them in a more honorable location.
Lucian asked who was speaking to him, and he identified himself as Gamaliel, Paul's teacher (see Acts 22:3). Gamaliel had
been secretly baptized in his lifetime. After death, he was buried
in this unfitting place along with Stephen and Gamaliel's
nephew, Nicodemus, the same one who visited Jesus by night
(see John 3). Nicodemus was later baptized by Peter and John.
This so angered Nicodemus' fellow members of the Sanhedrin,
they would have killed him except for the intervention of Gamaliel on his behalf. Instead they deposed him and beat him,
leaving him to die. Gamaliel took him to his own home where

he died a few days later. He buried him in his family tomb at the feet of St. Stephen, whom Gamaliel had also buried after his murderers left his body for the beasts and birds. The fourth person in Gamaliel's tomb was his son, Abibas, who was baptized at the age of twenty. His wife Ethea and his other son, Selimus, did not seek baptism, so were buried elsewhere. With this the dream ended, and Lucian awoke.

He prayed to God to confirm the divine origin of his dream by sending it a second and third time. The following Friday, Gamaliel returned in Lucian's dream and asked why Lucian did not inform Bishop John. Lucian explained that he asked God to confirm his experience by sending the dream a second time. In this second dream, Gamaliel told Lucian what he would find in the tombs: red roses for Stephen the martyr; white roses for Gamaliel and Nicodemus; and the fourth tomb with saffron for Abibas who died a virgin. The third week, Gamaliel appeared in Lucian's dream quite irate. He scolded Lucian for the delay. But now Lucian was convinced the dream was of God.

The next day, Lucian informed Bishop John and the other bishops. Even before they began digging at the indicated location, the air was filled with such fragrance that Lucian thought he was in paradise. Immediately seventy-three people were healed, demons fled in terror, hemorrhages ceased, fevers subsided, and many other miracles took place. The legend also reports that a stone found in the tomb recorded Stephen's Hebrew name: *kelil*, which means "crown" or "wreath," and is translated into Greek as *stephanos*. The finding of these relics by Lucian is commemorated on September 15th.

Stephen's bones were then reburied at the Sion Church which until AD 335 had been the bishop's residence in Jerusalem. The origins of this church might reach back to AD 130, but if so, it was likely destroyed by Diocletian in AD 303. It was subsequently reconstructed as the erroneously presumed location of the Upper Room (= Cenacle) of the Apostles and named "The Upper Church of the Apostles." In the fifth century, the church was renamed as "Sion, Mother of all the Churches."[8]

Yet the bones did not rest here. Instead they began to travel far and wide. The reason for the wide ranging journeys of these now divided bones was the belief that bones of holy people were an avenue to power.[9] Thus royal, priestly, or monastic persons who controlled bones became highly desirable patrons. Such a patron was in a position to connect needy—usually poor—people with the saints whose bones they possessed. As one might expect, those who possessed the bones took pride in their holdings and competed with others similarly blessed. One such person was the wife of Emperor Theodosius II, Eudocia, who competed over relics with her friend, Melania, a saintly married woman. This is a complex relationship to unravel, but it seems that Eudocia visited Melania in Jerusalem and returned home in 439 bringing some of Stephen's bones from Palestine to Constantinople. Eventually she placed them in the church of Saint Lawrence there. This is commemorated on August 3rd in the Western church.

Subsequently, Eudocia built a basilica to St. Stephen in Palestine that was dedicated in June 460. Excavations in the late nineteenth century uncovered the complete plan of this church. A new basilica was dedicated in 1900 and forms part of the École Biblique et Archéologique Française founded in 1890 by French members of the Order of Preachers (the Dominicans). The church is located some two hundred meters north of the Damascus gate along Nablus road. In October 460, Empress Eudocia died and was buried in a tomb she erected for herself next to the basilica of St. Stephen. By the sixth century, this place where Stephen's relics were kept became confused with the place where he was stoned. The myth continued well into the Middle Ages.

As anyone familiar with ancient "history" might suspect, there is another report, this one from the ninth century by Theophanes Confessor, with a different version of the transfer of the right arm of Stephen to Constantinople.[10]

> Under the influence of the blessed Pulcheria, the pious
> Theodosius sent a rich donation to the archbishop of Jeru-

salem for distribution to the needy, and also a golden cross studded with precious stones to be erected on Golgotha. In exchange for these gifts, the archbishop dispatched relics of the right arm of Stephen Protomartyr, in the care of St. Passarion. When this man had reached Chalcedon, in that very night the blessed Pulcheria saw St. Stephen in a vision saying to her: "Behold, your prayer has been heard and your desire has come to pass, for I have arrived in Chalcedon." And she arose taking her brother with her and went to greet the holy relics. Receiving them into the palace, she founded a splendid chapel for the holy Protomartyr, and in it she deposited the holy relics.

Pulcheria was the sister of Theodosius, who was young when he became emperor. To retain power, an emperor should have been victorious in battle, but Theodosius hadn't done that. Pulcheria was concerned about this, so she convinced her two sisters to join her in taking a vow of virginity. This precluded pretenders to Theodosius' throne from seeking to marry one of the sisters and usurp his power. But the vow bestowed great power on the women, for now they were of God, who would side with them in any battle their brother might undertake. Who would dare attack Theodosius? It was in this context of enhancing power that this legend concerning Pulcheria developed. Since she obtained a relic of St. Stephen and had it enshrined in Constantinople in AD 421, her power with God was fortified. Scholars differ as to which of these legends is authentic, but opinion favors Eudocia (in 439) rather than Pulcheria (in 421) as the one who brought Stephen's relics to Constantinople.

Parallels between Jesus and Stephen

Careful analysis of Luke's report about Stephen reveals interesting parallels with the trial and death of Jesus. Scholars have offered a variety of detailed reports, but here is a simplified schematic comparison that suits our purposes:

Event	Jesus	Stephen
Challenge opponents	Luke 20:1-7	Acts 6:9
Arrest	Luke 22:54	Acts 6:2
Trial before the Sanhedrin	Luke 22:66-71	Acts 6:12–15
False witnesses	not in Luke; Mark 14:56	Acts 6:13
Location of murder: outside the city	Luke 23:32	Acts 7:58
Martyr's death	Luke 23:32 (crucifixion)	Acts 7:58 (stoning)
Final words: "accept my spirit"	Luke 23:46	Acts 7:59
Forgive murderers	Luke 23:34	Acts 7:60
Son of Man saying	Luke 22:69	Acts 7:56
Immediate salvific effect	Luke 23:39-43	Acts 8:1, 4

What is a reader to make of these parallels? As already noted, fact and interpretation are not clearly separated in ancient history as is expected in modern historiography. The fact is that Stephen was tried and executed. But Luke's report of those events in Stephen's life was patterned after the experience of Jesus as Luke recorded it in his gospel. Neyrey[11] reminds readers that Luke is a historian in the Graeco-Roman mode. Interpreted history is what they wrote. Neyrey's contribution to understanding Luke's report about Stephen is that his trial is part of Luke's overall report of trials in the gospel and in Acts. Jesus' trials reflect Luke's basic pattern. Jesus is on trial four times in the gospel: before the Sanhedrin (Luke 22:66-71); before Pilate (Luke 23:1-5); before Herod (Luke 23:6-12); and before the assembled crowds of Judeans (Luke 23:13-25). These four trial reports help Luke to develop themes that will be repeated in the trials of others. Neyrey suggests considering these four reports as a unity (The Trial of Jesus).

A key element that Luke wants to highlight is Israel's rejection of God's prophets (Luke 6:22-23; 11:47-51; 13:33-34; 20:10-15; Acts 7:51-53). This applied to Jesus (Luke 6:7, 11; 7:31-35; 10:13-16; 11:47-51; 13:33-34; 19:14, 17; 20:10-15) and to Stephen (Acts 6:11-14). A further insight of Neyrey's on Luke's use of trials in his work is that Jesus predicts future trials for the church (Luke 12:8-12 and 21:12-15) and this is fulfilled in the trials of major figures in Acts: Peter, Stephen, and Paul. The trials take place in all the major places where Luke's gospel is preached (Judea, Jerusalem, Achaia, and Rome). They occur before Israelite courts as well as Roman tribunals. Sadly, the Israelite trials of Peter and the trials of Paul before Felix (Acts 21–24) and Festus (Acts 25–26) conclude with a final verdict.

Stephen's trial fulfills the pattern foretold by Jesus (Luke 21:12-15). He was prosecuted (Acts 6–7) and delivered up to a synagogue (Acts 6:9) and the Sanhedrin (Acts 6:12). Filled with the Holy Spirit, Stephen delivers a powerful witness on behalf of Jesus (Acts 6:10//Luke 12:11-12 and 21:14-15. The opponents are unable to withstand or refute his testimony (Acts 6:10//Luke 21:15). Their decision to put Stephen to a violent death is an admission of defeat. In Middle Eastern culture, the one who resorts to violence loses the argument.

Perhaps the most important contribution Neyrey makes to understanding the trials in Luke-Acts is that they all constitute one trial of Jesus. In other words, the trials have a double character. Jesus' trials in Luke's gospel and the trials of the apostles are trials of Israel. It was Israel who sat in judgment on Jesus and rejected his witness. This Israel judged itself guilty of false judgment in its rejection of God's prophet, Jesus. But in Luke's understanding, this trial was premature, and the trial should continue. Indeed it does in Acts of the Apostles. At the trials of Peter, Stephen, and Paul in Acts, Israel continues to hear witness about Jesus but continues to reject it all, thus increasing its guilt.

Neyrey has shed bright light on Luke and his compositions. The reader can understand Luke's intentions and the literary strategies he employed to communicate them. We understand now much better that Luke's report about Stephen is fact and interpretation. Like Jesus, Stephen was a real person who really existed and died. The tradition about the discovery of his bones appears to assure us of this. Whether Stephen died the way Luke reports is open to discussion. Even if there is a factual basis for the entire account, it is very heavily embellished or interpreted by Luke to fit his story line.

Social Science Approaches

Since the publication of his research on the parallels between Luke's gospel and Acts in 1995, Neyrey, along with many biblical scholars, has added a new tool to his interpreter's kit: social science methods. For more than twenty years, the Context Group of biblical scholars has been focusing on the ancient, Middle Eastern cultural context in which the Bible, its authors, and characters ought to be situated in order to be respectfully understood and interpreted. The tool is actually multifaceted since it includes a range of social sciences: Mediterranean anthropology, cultural anthropology, psychological anthropology, cognitive neuroscience, shamanistic studies, and many more.

In 1993, the Pontifical Biblical Commission published a document on the *Interpretation of the Bible in the Church* that summarized and evaluated the various methods used by biblical scholars in their research.[12] The centerpiece, the historical critical method, can be usefully supplemented with other methods. Among approaches that use the "human sciences," (from a Latin phrase more commonly translated in English as "the humanities"), the document approvingly includes the approach through cultural anthropology. It is widely known that the three paragraphs in this section reflect papers delivered by Context Group members at an International Meeting in Medina del Campo, Spain, in May, 1991.[13] As a founding member of that group, I am experienced in social science methods and eager to apply them to the biblical data concerning Stephen, one of the Seven.

Being the high-context documents that they are, all the books of the Bible presume that readers will supply the appropriate cultural information necessary for a complete understanding of what the documents meant to their intended audiences. It is not that the writers made incomplete reports. Rather, the writer presumes that he and the readers share the same language, culture, and perspectives. Why belabor the obvious? When readers do not share the same specific Mediterranean language, culture, and perspectives with the writer, miscommunication, misunderstanding, and misinterpretation will result. Social scientists try to provide some of the context that is necessary for readers who don't share the language, culture, or perspectives to interpret the texts.

For example, the author of Genesis 24 ("J") presumes the readers of his account of how Abraham's servant found the appropriate marriage partner for Isaac, his master's son, share the same language, culture, and perspective. Specifically, he confidently assumes the reader knows the strategy a Mediterranean person uses in order to obtain a favor from another Mediterranean person. He assumes the reader understands the rules of Mediterranean hospitality. Rebekah's brother, Laban, transforms the stranger-servant into a guest (Gen 24:31-32). Next, food is set before the servant who replies: "I will not eat until I have told my errand" (Gen 24:33).

To a Westerner who has followed the story to this point, such an act sounds rude and ungrateful. A Mediterranean person, however, understands what the servant is up to. He will not eat until he receives an answer to his request that Rebekah accompany him back to marry Isaac, for they are kin ideally related in this culture to be husband and wife (a parallel cousin, i.e., Isaac's mother's brother's daughter). He concludes his request by saying in effect: "Well? Yes or no? Let me know what my next course of action should be" (Gen 24:49). Laban and Bethuel (Rebekah's father) agree to the favor (Gen 24:52), and the servant and companions eat, drink, and spend the night (Gen 24:54).

No Bible to my knowledge, nor even any commentary familiar to me, interprets the story in this way. Yet an Iraqi student in class one semester said this is how any Middle Easterner would understand the story. It was an interpretation he shared with fellow students.

Conclusion

We can agree that Stephen was a person who really existed and died for his faith in Jesus Messiah as Luke reports and tradition has maintained. Yet as we read, we must keep ever in mind that Luke offers an interpretation of Stephen and his experiences. Luke is a high-context author of a high-context document who challenges modern Western readers to bring appropriate Middle Eastern cultural information to the task. That is what we aim to provide in this little book.

In chapter 1, we will reflect upon Stephen as a Hellenist, a "Greek." We have already given a brief definition of Hellenism above. Now we must probe the significance of this, especially as it helps to understand the tension experienced by the Hellenists regarding the neglect of Hellenist widows by the "Hebrews" (devout Judeans), notably the Twelve. In chapter 2, we seek further understanding of Benedict XVI's insistence that Stephen and his companions were not deacons. We will explore the evidence for that statement. Further, we will identify the role and function that the apostles created and recognized for the Seven in the community of believers: namely, commissioned ministers. A basic requirement for this ministry was that the candidate should be a "holy" person.

In chapter 3, we will try to understand why Luke refers to groups (the Seven, the Twelve) even as he focuses on individuals in these groups (Stephen, Philip, Peter, et al.). The key to understanding this lies in grasping the notion of collectivistic cultures and collectivistic personalities. This may be especially challenging for Western readers who in general are individualists, a person-type representing no more than twenty percent of the population on the planet. If collectivistic persons populate the pages of the Bible, individualists will be baffled and tempted to erroneously interpret them as fellow individualists. However, understanding Stephen and his companions as collectivistic persons will help understand why they—and the Twelve, too—were so concerned about needy persons in the group, and that the group should exist in peace and harmony (Acts 2:42).

The fourth and final chapter will return to a consideration of Stephen and his companions as holy persons (introduced in chapter 3). The holy person has direct contact with the spirit realm and brokers favors from that realm to humans on earth. Contact with God and spirits is ordinarily made in alternate states of consciousness (see 1 Sam 3:1). Luke's Greek vocabulary makes it clear that Stephen entered this level of mental awareness at the end of his speech. In fact, Luke mentions such experiences more than twenty times in the Acts of the Apostles. We will focus on alternative states of consciousness to cast Stephen in yet another light that receives little attention.

At the end, the reader should have a fresh understanding of Luke's interpretation of Stephen and his companions. This understanding will differ from traditional views, because it will have a very high degree of Middle Eastern cultural plausibility. Readers who desire a more theological or spiritual understanding are encouraged to draw inspiration from Pope Benedict XVI, who based his own reflections on the sketch of Stephen's life and ministry produced by historical critical biblical research. It is this very same outline which serves as the framework of this book.

John J. Pilch
Georgetown University
Washington, D.C.

Feast of the Stigmata of St. Francis of Assisi
September 17, 2007

CHAPTER 1

Stephen, a Hellenist

Luke introduces Stephen to his audience as one of seven "Hellenists" appointed by the Twelve to help redress a grievance about the (mis)treatment of "Hellenist" widows by the Hebrews. In general, Hellenists were Israelites enculturated in Greek values, language, and customs, while the Hebrews were devout Israelites who spoke the Aramaic language and were committed to the piety and customs of Judea. In Roman usage, Hellenists were considered cultivated, civilized people, and all others were barbarians. Luke's contrast between Hellenists and Hebrews is identical with Paul's contrast between Greeks and Judeans (Rom 3:9; 1 Cor 1:22-24; 10:32; 12:13). In their usage, both terms refer to categories of Israelites.

In this instance reported in Acts, the Hellenists were a Jerusalemite Jesus group who spoke (very likely only) Greek and prayed and recited their Scriptures in Greek, using a translation of the Bible called the Septuagint. Hellenists were a minority in Jerusalem. The Hebrews were a Jerusalemite Jesus group that might also have been able to speak some Greek, since it was widely spoken in first-century Palestine. They preferred, however, to speak and pray in Aramaic and recite their Scriptures in

Hebrew as best they could. They obviously constituted the majority in Jerusalem. Since the Hellenists and Hebrews in Jerusalem referred to were Israelites, the distinction between them in Acts is linguistic rather than ethnic. As previously noted, Paul calls these categories of Israelites "Judean" and "Greek" (Rom 3:9; 1 Cor 1:22-24 and throughout the letters). Given the fact that the Jesus group described here was Jerusalemite, living in the heart of Judean culture and values, the "Hebrews" would be right at home, while the "Hellenists" would be outsiders of sorts, hence the friction between them.

The Hellenistic Period

To fully understand the difference between Luke's Hellenists and Hebrews, it is necessary to appreciate the impact that the conquests of Alexander the Great (333 BC) had on peoples he subjected to his rule. It goes without saying that any conqueror spreads his language and culture. Alexander was no exception. In fact, he was so successful that some historians named the period from 300 BC to AD 300 the Hellenistic period.

Though 1–2 Maccabees and Daniel create the impression that Israelites resisted Greek rule and Hellenization, it is more likely that Israelites held different views as to how far one could or should assimilate while holding on to one's traditions. Under Antiochus Epiphanes IV Jerusalemite priests aspired to Hellenistic citizenship for themselves, something from which they retreated after the success of the Maccabees. In contrast others, particularly in the Diaspora, were willing to interact with Hellenistic culture but did not want to be tainted by it. In any case, Hellenistic influence was difficult to resist, much less avoid completely. What must be kept in mind is that the word "Hellenist" when applied to Israelites covers a wide range of attitudes toward and acceptance of Greek culture. "Hellenist" does not describe a monolithic entity sharing a unified understanding of this term.

The Septuagint

One of the first consequences for Israelites after the conquests by Alexander was the need for a Greek translation of their Scripture. Through the period of the Babylonian captivity (587–537 BC), Aramaic, the official language of the Babylonian Empire, continued as the language of the Israelites, while Hebrew became the book language of the educated few. The Bible in Hebrew was meant to keep the biblical tradition out of the reach of the majority nonelite, even apart from the fact that the vast majority were illiterate. The Aramaic language prevailed through the Persian period as well (537 to 300 BC). In fact, Aramaic remained an important language for Israelites for centuries afterward, notably in the Eastern Diaspora. The Targumim (plural of Targum), that is, Aramaic paraphrases of the Hebrew Scriptures, flourished in the first seven centuries AD because this was the language familiar to and spoken by ordinary Israelites. In Palestine it remained the preferred language even in the Hellenistic period when many were familiar with Greek.

As for the Greek language, legend has it that around 282 BC, at the invitation of Ptolemy (Philadelphus II [285–247 BC]), seventy-two mythical translators came to Egypt and were to have rendered their Torah into Greek in seventy-two days. Ptolemy intended this translation primarily for "outsiders" as an aid to learning more about these "foreign" people in Alexandria. Of course, Israelites themselves also benefitted, since Greek replaced Aramaic as the language of the empire. Over the next three centuries other portions of the Hebrew Bible were translated into Greek. In fact, in the prologue to his translation of his grandfather's book (*Ben Sira* or *Sirach*, around 116 BC) from Hebrew to Greek, the grandson expressed the same intention: "to help outsiders," though he admitted translation was difficult. By the second century AD (Justin Martyr and Irenaeus), the entire Greek translation (the Septuagint) was credited to the seventy-two and read by Jesus groups. For their part, Pharisees reacted negatively to this acceptance of the Septuagint by Jesus groups and discouraged its use among Israelites. They produced fresh Greek translations of their Scriptures (e.g., Aquila, in AD 128, or Symmachus around AD 180–192).

The Septuagint contains the standard thirty-nine books of the Hebrew Bible as well as certain apocryphal books. The term "apocrypha" was coined by St. Jerome in the fifth century and referred in general to ancient Israelite writings produced during the period after Malachi (Persian period) until the time of Jesus. The apocryphal books include Judith, Tobit, Baruch, Ben Sira (also called Sirach, or Ecclesiasticus), the Wisdom of Solomon, 1–2 Maccabees, the two books of Esdras, additions to the book of Esther, additions to the book of Daniel, and the Prayer of Manasseh.

Two "Diasporas"

Israelites were exiled from the land early in their history. Shalmaneser V (727–722 BC) carried Israelites away from Samaria to Assyria (2 Kings 17:6). There were other periods of exile in subsequent centuries, but can one really speak of Diasporas or dispersions? Israeli social scientists Edrei and Mendels choose these terms.[1] Yet in the perception of Israelites of the first century AD, there was no forced dispersion of Judeans across the Mediterranean and the Middle East. As Philo claims, Judeans around the Mediterranean formed "colonies." He says this in reflections on Jerusalem:

> As for the holy city, I must say what befits me to say. While she, as I have said, is my native city she is also the mother city [*metropolis*] not of one country Judaea but of most of the others in virtue of *the colonies sent out at diverse times* to the neighboring lands Egypt, Phoenicia, the part of Syria called the Hollow and the rest as well as the lands lying far apart, Pamphylia, Cilicia, most of Asia up to Bithynia and the corners of Pontus, similarly also into Europe, Thessaly, Boeotia, Macedonia, Aetolia, Attica, Argos, Corinth and most of the best part of Peloponnese. (emphasis added) (*Gaius* 281; see also *Flaccus* 46)

Moreover, many of those who were exiled or left voluntarily had no intention of ever returning. Stephen and his companions belonged to such a Hellenistic colony or colonies of the Hellenistic period. Except for Nicolaus, though, we don't know where the colonies of the other six were. Israelites in these colonies read or heard their Bible in Greek translation. The contrast between Hellenists and Hebrews during this period was evident in some of these apocryphal books in the Septuagint. For example, on the one hand, the author of the Wisdom of Solomon who wrote in very polished Greek seems to hide his Israelite identity and strives to present himself convincingly as a Hellenist. Still, his book evinces unbending loyalty to the Torah and an ever-ready willingness to suffer for Torah's sake (Wis 3:1-9). Yet reflective of his Hellenistic orientation, he claims the Torah is true, divine wisdom for all human beings (Wis 18:4).

This first century AD division among Israelites (Hellenists and Hebrews, Greeks and Judeans) clearly had strong linguistic roots in its past. Yet the division was also rooted in geography.[2] In the Hellenistic era, the Israelite departure from Palestine was both sizeable and geographically widespread. The Eastern segment extended from Transjordan to Babylonia (roughly modern Jordan to Iraq-Iran). The Western segment included Asia Minor (the western section of modern Turkey), modern Greece, Italy, and the Mediterranean islands. Palestine was the "border" between these two segments, though as Acts and other portions of the New Testament seem to indicate, some Israelites in Palestine such as Jerusalem did write and speak Greek. We deduce this from Greek synagogue inscriptions, such as the Theodotus Inscription from Jerusalem dated from before AD 70.[3] Synagogue inscriptions in the West are all in Greek, while synagogue inscriptions in Palestine were written in Greek, Aramaic, and Hebrew. According to John (19:20), the title above Jesus' head on the cross was written in Hebrew (= Aramaic), Latin, and Greek.

The Bible, of course, was the common Scripture of each community, but each had access to it in a different language. In the West (the colonies from which Stephen and his Hellenist companions came and to which Paul brought the good news), the Septuagint with the Apocrypha was their Bible. It is the text reflected in New Testament allusions, references, and "quotations." Some documents of the Septuagint were originally written in Greek (e.g., Wis, 2 Macc), others were translated from Hebrew to Greek (e.g., 1 Macc). The Western tradition, however, was essentially written! In the East, Hebrew Scriptures that were recited or read in the community center (the synagogue) were then paraphrased orally in the Aramaic language for the audience by the translator (metarguman).

The written Targumim record these Aramaic paraphrases. At present, we have Targum texts to all the books of the Hebrew Bible except for Ezra, Nehemiah, and Daniel. Though some Targumim are rather literal (e.g., Targum Onkelos; the Targum of Job found at Qumran and dating from the first century BC), most are paraphrases or include huge amounts of material with a slim or no basis in the text (e.g., the Targum to the Song of Songs). Still other traditions were transmitted orally. For instance, Mark's Jesus challenged the oral tradition of the elders about washing cups and pots and bronze vessels (Mark 7:3-5) as well as the oral tradition about *qorban* (Mark 7:9-13), neither of which has a basis in the Bible. This oral tradition—especially in Aramaic—flourished in Palestine but didn't transfer to the colonies in the West. This helps understand why Mark has to explain the tradition and translate Aramaic phrases (*talitha kumi*, Mark 5:41) even though he is writing for Israelites.

The colonies in the East and in the West strove to maintain their Israelite identity and their connection to Jerusalem, the center, the location of the temple of the God of Israel. At the same time, Israelites in the colonies needed to integrate into the broader cultural setting in which they lived. This was a struggle requiring a balance that was not easy to achieve. For example, some Israelite traditions concerning agriculture, working the land, purity laws and concerns about impurity, and temple services that made sense in Palestine were simply irrelevant in the West. There is no evidence for ritual baths (*mikva*) in the Western colonies. From the so-called Council of Jerusalem in Acts 15, we realize that Israelites in the Western colonies did not practice circumcision. Many Israelites living among non-Israelite Hellenistic populations considered it barbaric mutilation. Moreover, circumcision that was first introduced in Israel around 150 BC consisted in a nick which could easily be made to look like non-circumcision if the need arose.[4] This is the meaning of Paul's comments concerning "removing the marks of circumcision" (1 Cor 7:18). It was only after the Bar Kochba revolt (after AD 135) that circumcision involved removal of the entire foreskin. The Western colonies also did not observe food restrictions. This is why the East firmly believed that the Torah could not be fulfilled outside of Palestine.

The Synagogue

Stephen's opponents were fellow Hellenists (Greek-speaking Israelites) from the "synagogue of the Freedmen" (Acts 6:9). It is not clear from the text whether the reference is to a single "synagogue" attended by Freedmen, Cyrenians, Alexandrians, and men from Cilicia and Asia, or to several "synagogues," one for each of these groups named. Though many scholars favor a single synagogue, resolving this problem is not as important as understanding what "synagogue" means. Contemporary Bible readers no doubt think the word refers to a building, specifically a place of worship. They don't pause to consider that while the temple was standing, there could really be no other place of worship, because there was no need for one. Ignoring this, modern Christians further tend to assume that early Jesus groups adopted practices and structures from the synagogue in developing their own worship. In actuality, the process may have worked in reverse. Synagogue worship services appear to have developed as a reflection of Israelite Jesus group practices.[5]

Thus it is a legitimate question to ask whether the term "ancient synagogues"—of which we have only fragmentary and enigmatic remains—actually referred to a building, or a function, or the people who gathered in a place for a variety of purposes (McKay). In other words, since literary evidence indicates that Israelite males gathered in "synagogues" usually on the Sabbath in our period, one can ask a series of questions. Were these meetings called "the synagogue"? Or was the group called "the synagogue"? Or was the open space, the room, or the building in which the room was located called "the synagogue"? The questions probe the nature and function of the people, building complexes, or institutions which through the centuries have been called "synagogues" indiscriminately.

Archaeologists are still not able to distinguish these fragmentary remains from domestic buildings of the same period. Thus attributing functions to these remains is an anachronistic or ethnocentric retrojection of later views to antiquity. As for assigning a specific religious function to these buildings, it is necessary to distinguish Sabbath observance from Sabbath worship. Sabbath observance involves rest and refraining from work and trading on the Sabbath (Exod 20:8-11). This has a long history in Israel. Sabbath worship, in contrast, involves purposeful, communal activity directed to the God of Israel with the intention of worship. Scholars believe such worship developed only after the destruction of the second temple. Even then, the development took quite a long time, perhaps more than one hundred years.

The Theodotus inscription (mentioned above) offers some insight about first-century "synagogues."

> Theodotus, son of Quettenos (Vettenos), priest and archi-synagogus, son of an archisynagogus, grandson of an archisynagogus, built this synagogue for the reading of the law and for the teaching of the commandments, and the hostel and the chambers and the water fittings for the accommodation of those who [coming] from abroad have need of it, of which [synagogue] the foundations were laid by his fathers and the Elders and the Simonides.[6]

Here, the word "synagogue" clearly refers to a building. But what was the purpose or function of this building? And if the reference is to a building, how does the archisynagogus (leader or president of a synagogue) relate to it? Does he preside over the building like a caretaker or superintendent? Or does he rather preside like a chairperson over the assembly that meets in the building? The inscription makes no mention of regular communal prayer services. Regular communal daily prayers became part of the synagogue's operation only after AD 70. While the gospels and other sources mention Sabbath services, it is not clear what these services entailed, and still less whether they were worship services. The inscription mentioned "reading of the Law and teaching the commandments." Study was thus one major activity that took place in this building, but unless it was part of a worship service (which we don't know for certain), such study served mainly to preserve and strengthen group identity. Notice that the building offered lodging for Diaspora travelers to Jerusalem and perhaps others. Some synagogues had facilities for serving meals. The building also served as a meeting hall for community business, for local law courts that disciplined offenders, or as a place for debate and argumentation. In other words, if "synagogue" refers to a building, it is a multifunction building and not primarily or even necessarily a place of worship. The suggestion that the Theodotus inscription refers to the synagogue of Freedmen is debated, but not very probable.

McKay believes the synagogue eventually became a place of worship long after the destruction of the temple (perhaps first by AD 200), and this in conscious imitation of similar developments among Israelite Jesus groups. She proposes as the most secure meaning for ancient synagogues "a committee of Israelite men who managed their community's affairs." These committees exercised various civic, religious and educational functions as required. Thus, the "synagogue of the Freedmen" (whether the reference is to one or many) refers to a group or groups of Israelite men who gathered for a variety of reasons.

The Hellenist group that disputed with Stephen the Hellenist was quite disparate in composition (Acts 6:9). Notice that even Hellenists disagreed with each other. They were not a monolithic group. Some scholars believe that "Freedmen" identified some of these Hellenists as emancipated Israelites (or their descendants) who were taken to Rome as slaves by Pompey in 63 BC. Cyrenians were Hellenistic Israelites from Cyrene in northern Africa. While these Cyrenians took issue with Stephen in part over Jesus, other Cyrenian Hellenists preached Jesus to fellow Hellenists in Antioch (Acts 11:20). Alexandrians were Hellenistic Israelites from Egypt. Alexandria had a large Greek-speaking Israelite population. Recall that it was there that the Septuagint was translated. Cilicia and Asia refer to two areas of Asia Minor (western Turkey). Cilicia was an area on the southern coast, and Asia bordered the Aegean Sea.

All of these Hellenistic Israelites hailing from colonies in different regions of the world would certainly gather for mutual support in a community center or men's club in Jerusalem. Whether in one place or in five different places, they would enjoy the company of those who like themselves (perhaps) spoke only Greek. As Israelites from the western colonies, they cherished the Septuagint, the Greek translation of their Scriptures. Beyond the common language, however, these Israelites were thoroughly acculturated to Hellenism. It was not only the language, but also the culture and customs of Hellenism that bound them together. Still, relative to the Stephen report, it is important to remember that these Hellenists may have experienced different levels of acculturation. As is evident from their reaction to Stephen's speech, their attachment to Israelite practices, especially regarding the temple, seems to have differed significantly among them.

Stephen's Speech[7]

Scholars believe the basic and original story about Stephen extended from Acts 6:1 to Acts 7:1 ("And the high priest said,

'Is this so?'") and then continued in Acts 7:54 ("Now when they heard these things they were enraged . . ."). The speech (Acts 7:2–53), which in its present form is most definitely a Lucan composition (even though he likely inherited it, perhaps from an Antiochene tradition), had been inserted into a story about the lynching of Stephen. He was the first Jesus group member to die for witnessing to Jesus. While it is often presented as a defense speech, Stephen does not reply to the charges: blasphemy against Moses and God (6:11), attacks on the temple and the law (6:13), and claiming that Jesus will destroy this place and change the customs Moses gave (6:14). In fact, at its center, his speech openly attacks temple-centered worship (vv. 44-50) and implicit in that is an attack on the law (v. 38).

From a cultural perspective, it is preferable to interpret the charges against Stephen as a challenge to his honor. Stephen is accused of dishonoring the temple because he said that Jesus would destroy the temple and change Mosaic custom (Acts 6:13-14). What our high-context document omits is that the risen Jesus would do these things when he returns soon to establish a new theocratic political religious system, the kingdom of God. Stephen has a cultural obligation to respond to this challenge. Should he fail to respond or fail to give a resounding rebuttal of the charges, the challenge will have succeeded in shaming him. If the "original story" did not record his response, tradition and Luke would create a plausible and winning response.

The speech as we have received it can be divided into two parts: a selective history of Israel (vv. 2-50) and a comparison of past Israelite behavior with present conduct (vv. 51-53). It is crafted according to two cultural perspectives crucial to Stephen's defense. For the most part, Stephen relies on the cultural adage that "the son is like the father!" (See Acts 7:51 and compare Matt 11:27; Sir 30:1; Deut 23:2; Isa 57:3; Hos 1:2). The selective history of Stephen's speech highlights three ancestors: Abraham (vv. 2b-8a), Joseph (vv. 9-16), and Moses (vv. 20-38). Stephen's point is the "brethren and fathers" (Acts 7:2) who challenge his statements about Jesus raised by God from the dead are just like their forefathers who killed the prophets (Acts 7:52-53); of twenty-eight occurrences of the word "fathers" in Acts, thirteen appear in Stephen's speech!

A key element in this speech occurs for the first time in the Abraham segment. At God's direction, Abraham wanders from Ur to Haran and finally settles in Canaan. Stephen refers to Canaan as "this place" (7:7), where Israel—after its liberation from Egypt—would serve Yahweh. Eventually "place" will refer to the temple, but this first occurrence which does not is significant for the rest of his argument. The argument will boil down to this: in what "place" can a person serve Yahweh? Where is the appropriate "place"?

In the Joseph segment, Stephen recounts how Jacob and his family got to Egypt during the famine. He notes that Jacob and his family died there but were buried in Canaan. The speech confuses land purchased by Jacob at Shechem (Gen 33:19) where Joseph was buried (Josh 24:32) with the burial place purchased by Abraham near Hebron (Gen 23:16-20) where Jacob, Abraham, Sarah, Isaac, Rebekah, and Leah were buried. Josephus (Ant. 2.8.2, par. 199) says that Joseph's brothers were also buried in Hebron. While such inconsistencies greatly concern modern readers, they obviously were not significant to the ancient writers and their audiences who may or may not have known what we do. The important point for Stephen's speech is that while Joseph spent much of his life in another land (Egypt) where God looked after him and his family, he and his family (and the patriarchs) were buried in the land of Canaan.

The third segment focuses on Moses whom some Hebrews rejected (7:27, 35) but God chose as their ruler and deliverer (7:35). God bestowed upon Moses the roles fellow Hebrews refused to acknowledge in him or accept from him. The significance of Moses for Stephen the Hellenist's speech is that he was foreign born and educated, yet pleasing to God ("Moses was born, and was beautiful before God" [7:20]). The speech also recasts the person of Moses who described himself as "slow of speech and of tongue" (Exod 4:10) into a man "mighty in his words and deeds" (Acts 7:22). The rest of Moses' story as reported in Exodus is similarly reinterpreted until the moment when God appears to Moses at the burning bush and commissions him to rescue the Hebrews from Egyptian bondage. This is an important building block in Stephen's speech concerning "holy ground" or "holy place." Neither Abraham nor Moses built a shrine or temple or offered sacrifice in order to encounter God. Wherever God appears is a holy place. One final important notice about Moses is his promise: "God will raise up for you a prophet from your brethren as he raised me up" (Acts 7:37). This notice will be important later as Stephen concludes his speech. However, the Moses segment is Stephen's answer to the charge that he blasphemed Moses (6:11).

Next follows two pieces of historical background (7:39-50) for two concluding accusations (vv. 51-53). The first piece of information concerns Israel's further rejection of Moses and its idolatry in the desert (39-43). They begged Aaron to make an image of a god who would lead them. To this image of a calf-god they offered sacrifice and thus rebelled against the God of their ancestors. The idea was that the god would appear over the calf and they would attempt to control the god. It is worth noting that this idea dies hard. Later in Israel's history, the God of Israel, Yahweh, was enthroned above the ark over two winged bulls (the cherubim) just like the calf mentioned here. Stephen's point is that Israel has a long history of rebellion against God. In addition, they worshiped the stars and constellations in the sky which the ancients considered to be living beings not pieces of rock. At this point, Stephen quotes Amos (5:25-27 in the Septuagint, which differs from the Hebrew) to remind his audience that God had punished Israel for this desert idolatry.

The second item of historical background (7:44-50) concerns the "tent of witness" made by God's command and design. It symbolized God's presence among the people as they continued toward Canaan. At this tent they paid homage to God. But Israel's kings replaced this with a temple made according to human plans. Stephen's point is the people preferred a human construct to what God had requested.

Having built up his case, Stephen now levels his accusations against his audience. First the settlement generation rejected the worship place revealed by God to Moses, the tent of witness, in favor of a temple built by human labor and expertise. Second, though Moses promised that the God of the fathers would always provide the people with prophets, spokespersons for God in their here-and-now, previous generations consistently killed God's chosen prophets. The present "brethren and fathers" continue the sins of their forefathers in the custom of killing God's prophets, notably Jesus (and shortly, Stephen himself).

Just as the cultural adage "like father, like son" shaped Stephen's pointed response to the challenge to his honor, a second cultural perspective shapes the conclusion to this speech. Qoheleth, the speaker in Ecclesiastes, expressed it thus: "there is nothing new under the sun" (Eccl 1:9). While God's raising of "the Righteous One" Jesus from the dead might seem to be something new, his treatment at the hands of the "brethren and fathers" who have now "betrayed and murdered" him is quite in line with the traditional story of Israel from Abraham to Stephen's present. Jesus is of the lineage of Abraham, a prophet like those foretold by Moses, and he was killed as a prophet quite in line with Israel's tradition of disobeying God and killing God's prophets.

As we noted, all Hellenists did not form a monolithic group sharing an identical belief system. What they shared in common was having lived or presently living outside of Israel as a minority group in Hellenistic colonies or locales. They were thus assimilated in varying degrees to Hellenistic culture while striving to retain some measure of Israelite identity. From the speech placed in Stephen's mouth by tradition and finessed by Luke, it is clear that Stephen does not view the temple and the practices associated with it as essential to Israelite identity. Prior to the destruction of the temple such an attitude, which was shared by other Hellenists, is noteworthy. It is also quite understandable when an Israelite lives far from the land of Israel and has little or no opportunity to make a pilgrimage there.

It is also clear from the speech that while Stephen holds Moses in high regard as an ancestor beloved by God (Acts 7:20), many of the "customs which Moses delivered to us" (Acts 6:14) are irrelevant (e.g., agricultural observances) and even viewed as barbaric (e.g., circumcision) in the wider Hellenistic world.

The response of the Sanhedrin was rage and a mob response to kill him for his blasphemy. Paul, at whose feet the murderers laid their garments, was a Hellenistic Israelite from the colony in Tarsus. He agreed with this deed. Though he was from a Hellenist colony, at this point of the story he totally disagreed with Stephen. Paul described himself thus: "circumcised on the eighth day, of the people of Israel, of the tribe of Benjamin, a Hebrew born of Hebrews; as to the law a Pharisee, as to zeal a persecutor of the church, as to righteousness under the law blameless" (Phil 3:5-6). In other words, he knew and wrote in the Greek language, and in his letters he relied on the Septuagint. He thus had first-hand familiarity with Hellenistic culture. Yet according to Acts, he could also speak Aramaic, and until shortly after Stephen's murder, as he himself admits, he was thoroughly a devout Israelite (= Hebrew) in his beliefs, convictions, and practices. It is very plausible to conclude that what Paul, a conservative Hellenist, learned about and perhaps from Stephen prepared him for the dramatic change in understanding that he underwent on the road to Damascus.

Conclusion

For Luke's original audience, it was sufficient for him to identify Stephen and his companions as Hellenists or Greeks. They were familiar with this division in the "house of Israel" long before the first century AD. Luke's readers could also understand how this division played out in the Judean and Hellenistic Jesus groups as they sought to live according to their experience of Jesus. This is a very high-context report, totally obscure for a contemporary Western reader. What we presented in this chapter is more information about this division and its respective segments, information which was known to Luke's original audience but not to us. With that we were able to understand Stephen's speech as a quintessential Hellenistic response to Judean concerns. Living in different parts of the world made coexistence easy for Hellenists and Judeans. Living together in Jerusalem brought their differences of opinion to the fore and resulted in conflicts. Stephen made a superb effort to refute his challengers with a well-crafted and delivered speech. The fact that they resorted to violence and put Stephen to death culturally indicates that they lost the argument. In Middle Eastern agonistic cultures, that is cultures inclined to debate, argumentation, confrontation, and the like, the first one who resorts to violence is judged to have admitted losing the argument. Stephen the Hellenist was successful, but he paid the price.

CHAPTER 2

Stephen, a Collectivist

Though he conducted the classical studies of the social pattern known as collectivism, the anthropologist Harry Triandis cautions that some societies view the concept negatively. It is often associated with dictatorial or totalitarian political systems. Even other anthropologists prefer words such as group-centered, socio-centric, holistic, allocentric, ensembled, constitutive, contextualist, connected, relational, and equivalent terms. We will use the standard technical term "collectivist" as defined by Triandis.[1]

The concept was introduced into biblical studies by Malina in his article on Ignatius of Antioch.[2] He and other colleagues continued to develop and apply the notion to many parts of the Bible.[3] By now thirty years later, the concept is probably familiar to many students of the Bible. Malina devoted a chapter to it in a companion volume in this series on Timothy. We will summarize the salient ideas particularly as they will help us to understand Stephen, one of the Seven.

Collectivists and Individualists

These concepts describe social patterns of interaction, both across cultures and within any given society. Indeed, the patterns can and do exist within each human person. To review the concepts,[4] collectivism can be described as a social pattern in which closely linked individuals perceive themselves primarily as parts of one or more collectives: family, coworkers, tribe, nation, the military, and so forth. These individuals are primarily motivated by the rules of as well as the duties imposed by these collectives. They are always ready to sacrifice their personal goals to the goals of the collectivity. They emphasize their connectedness to other members of these collectives. For example, members of the U.S. military often refer to their fellows as a "band of brothers."

In contrast, individualism is a social pattern in which very loosely linked individuals perceive themselves as totally independent of collectivities. Their primary motivation derives from their own preferences, needs, and rights, as well as the informal contracts they have established with others. The goals of the group or of others are always secondary to personal goals. They emphasize the need for rational analysis of the advantages and disadvantages of association with other individuals or groups.

One social scientist used driving an automobile as an illustration. In Manila, a collectivist society, traffic jams are colossal and are among the worst in the world, seemingly day and night. Yet even though the traffic creeps and signal lights are often disobeyed, accidents are very rare. Drivers do care for other drivers and pedestrians. The operation is collaborative rather than competitive. In individualist societies, for instance, New York City, traffic jams raise blood pressure and stir incessant horn blowing. Each driver competes to get ahead of the others, devil take the hindmost. Accident rates are quite high.

Social scientists note that eighty percent of the world's population is primarily collectivist in nature.[5] Many collectivists disagree with Western views, in which the twenty percent of the world's individualist population is found. While these percentages are confirmed by research, and "pure" versions of these social patterns do exist among many groups worldwide, such pure versions are undesirable and unhealthy for a group. Pure individualism boils down to selfishness, narcissism, anomie, high crime, high rates of divorce, and child abuse, among other social ills. Pure collectivism, especially in the context of hostility between groups (collectivities), results in ethnic cleansing, oppression of human rights, and exploitation of some ingroup members for the benefit of the entire ingroup.

In truth, the world's collectivists follow that social pattern in most situations in which they are dealing with the ingroup. When dealing with outgroups, collectivists act more like individualists. They attempt to maximize their benefits and outcomes at the expense of those in the outgroup. Such switching between collectivism and individualism occurs regularly, even within kin groups. An Arab proverb observes: "I against my brother. I and my brother against our cousin. I, my brother and my cousin, against the neighboring family." And so on. To avoid such shifting allegiances, collectivists strive to maintain very close relationships.

Scholars who frown on the word "collectivism" have introduced the notions of idiocentrism and allocentrism. Idiocentric people believe, feel, and behave the way individualists do around the world. They see themselves at the center of their universe. Allocentric people, on the other hand, believe, feel, and behave the way collectivists do around the world. And people always shift from one view to the other. Generally speaking, an American would readily and freely marry a partner of whom the parents do not approve. This is idiocentric behavior. On the other hand, parental approval is important for some Americans (allocentric), and they would search for a partner who pleased the parents. Thus, in every culture, there exists a full distribution of types.

To gain a better grasp of the contrast between individualists and collectivists, here is a chart that sketches the differences:[6]

Individualists, e.g., U.S. Citizens	Collectivists, e.g., Mediterraneans
egocentric identity: emphasis on "I"	group-centric identity: emphasis on "We"
promote independence	promote interdependence
see the parts	see the whole
urge uniqueness	urge conformity
seek autonomy from social solidarity	seek integration into social reality
primary responsibility to self and individual potential	primary obligation to others and the development of the group
group membership results from a renewable contract	group membership results from one's inherited social and familiar place in society
behavior is governed by rights and duties specified by one's personal goals	behavior is dictated by the group's mores and sanctions, or the leader's authority
individual worth is based on individual achievements or individual possessions	individual worth is rooted in inherited familial status, social position, class, or caste
status is achieved	status is ascribed
achieving and competing is a motivational necessity and the norm	achieving and competing is disruptive to the group
assert one's own rights	submit personal rights to the group
equality is a key value	hierarchy is a key value
friendships are functional	friendships involve long-term loyalties or obligational commitments
any group is viewed as only a collection of individuals	any group is viewed as an organismic unit, inextricably interlocked

(Continued)

Individualists, e.g., U.S. Citizens	Collectivists, e.g., Mediterraneans
the individual self is viewed as an entity separate from the physical world and from other persons	the individual self is viewed as organically connected with the physical world and with other persons
any personal decision is made by the self alone even if it is not in the group's best interests	any personal decision is made in consultation with the group and often in obedience or deference to its will
private autonomy	corporate solidarity
strong personal identity	strong familial identity
self-reliant achievement	interdependent collaboration
strong desire to be personally satisfied	strong desire to be interpersonally satisfying or satisfactory

Stephen, One of the Seven: a Collectivist

Luke's report about the tension between the Hebrews and the Hellenists (Acts 6:1-6) describes two groups or collectivities. As we noted in the previous chapter, the division between Hellenists and Hebrews reached further back into history than the first century AD. What is reported here in Acts 6 is not a new division in Judaism. Notice however, that no individuals are identified until seven Hellenists are selected to help resolve the issue. We will return to these named individuals later. For the moment, both Hebrews and Hellenists can be understood in terms of the characteristics listed in the right hand column above. They are collectivists. This is what they share in common as members of "the house of Israel" (Acts 2:36), and as such they form an ingroup relative to nonmembers of the house of Israel.

Ingroups are groups of individuals about whose welfare each member is concerned. In the ingroup, each member is willing to cooperate for the benefit of the group without demanding something in return. Separation from the ingroup leads to excruciating anxiety. Ingroup members have a sense of a shared fate. Ingroup members also don't hesitate to butt into the affairs of other members. In Jerusalem, however, the Hebrews of the house of Israel form an ingroup, while Hellenists in the house of Israel are the outgroup. The Hellenists concerned about their widows are obviously males. In Middle Eastern culture, a woman is always under the care of a male: father, husband, or son. Widows have lost their husbands. Their fathers might also be deceased. That leaves sons or kin to look after them. The Hellenists who lodge a grievance with the Hebrews are males concerned about members of their ingroup. While Hellenists constitute an ingroup of their own, they are an outgroup in Jerusalem, at the very least because of the language they speak (Greek) if not also the one they can't speak (Aramaic)! They feel they are being treated as an outgroup by the Hebrews.

The Hebrews in Jerusalem are definitely an ingroup. They are at home here. They care for their own with whom they share common beliefs, practices, and yes, a common language. The Hebrews continue to teach in Aramaic both in the temple and in private homes (Acts 2:46; 3:1; 5:19-21; 5:42). What can we say about their "neglect" of the Hellenist widows in the daily ministry? Collectivists in general hoard information even more than individualists do, and they do not share it with outgroups. Individualists hoard information because it is a key to their success and achievement, and depriving others of it assures superiority. Collectivist ingroups notoriously hide information from others to an even greater degree. One reason for this is concern for honor and reputation. If others in the group know too much about a person, how can that person make an honor claim or preserve a good reputation (deserved or not)? Hence secrecy, deception, and lying control the flow of information. While the Hebrew "neglect" of instructing Hellenist widows (more about this in the next chapter) is likely unintentional and not spiteful, it could also be intentional. It could plausibly be prompted by an intention to hoard firsthand, eyewitness knowledge from the Hellenists. Cooperation in collectivistic cultures occurs only within the ingroup. Extreme competition is used with outgroups.

Notice further in the chart above that behavior in a collectivist group is dictated by the group's mores and sanctions, or by the leader's authority. The Hellenists who spoke up on behalf of their widows were quite likely leaders in the group. Thus, the Hellenist leaders charged the Hebrew leaders (the Twelve) with neglect of duty toward these widows.

Granted, the Hellenist outgroup had its own meeting places (e.g., the synagogue of the Freedmen, Acts 6:9). Here they could discuss the Scriptures (among other things) in the Greek language: the Septuagint. But they held the Twelve in high esteem and would have appreciated receiving instruction from these eyewitnesses. Apparently none of the Hellenists had been eyewitnesses, because that is not one of the requirements for ministry postulated by the Twelve (Acts 6:3; compare Acts 1:21-22). However, the Twelve feel hindered in attending to the Hellenist widows by at least two things. One, they refuse to devote any less time to "preaching the word of God" (6:2) in the temple and private homes where Aramaic is the common language. Two, they may not have felt as competent to teach in the Greek language as the Hellenists would be. Hence the decision by the Twelve to commission Hellenist ministers who would be able to tend to the needs of Hellenists. Later in Acts (11:19-20), Luke seems to suggest that some of these ministers might have been competently bilingual. After being forced to flee from Jerusalem following Stephen's murder, some spoke to Hebrews in Phoenicia, Cyprus, and Antioch (11:19), presumably in Aramaic. Others from Cyprus and Cyrene spoke to Hellenists in Antioch (11:20).

It is possible to add yet another dimension to our consideration of collectivity, namely, a lineal orientation, a concern about hierarchy and authority. Every culture can choose from three options regarding how human beings relate to one another. The following chart compares these three options. Different options prevail in different cultures, and sometimes within a culture the options will be manifest in different groups in the culture. Here is another chart to facilitate reflection[7]:

INDIVIDUAL-CENTERED	GROUP-CENTERED	LINEAL-ORIENTED
egocentric identity	group-centric identity	tradition-, authority-centered identity
promotes independence	promotes interdependence	promotes obedience and respect
see the parts	see the whole	see the lineal sequence
autonomy from social solidarity	integration into social reality	find and maintain the right location in the social ladder or hierarchy
primary responsibility to self and individual potential	primary responsibility to others and development of the group	primary responsibility to authority or tradition, and being loyal to it
urges uniqueness	urges conformity	urges obedience
group membership results from a renewable contract	group membership results from one's inherited social and familial place in society; or accepting a call to a fictive-kin group	lineal membership results from genealogical pedigree, induction, seniority
behavior is governed by rights and duties determined by one's personal goals	behavior is dictated by the group's mores and sanctions	behavior is dictated by tradition and/or authority
individual worth is based on individual achievements or individual possessions	individual worth is rooted in familial status or group status	individual worth is rooted in social position, class, caste, rank, etc.
status is achieved	status is ascribed	status is ascribed: inherited or merited

(Continued)

INDIVIDUAL-CENTERED	GROUP-CENTERED	LINEAL-ORIENTED
achieving and competing is a motivational necessity and the norm	achieving and competing is disruptive; interdependent collaboration is the norm	vaunting one's prominence and authority is the norm
assert one's own rights	submit personal rights to the group	rights are delegated by authority or derived from the bloodline
equality is a key value	relative equality is a key value	hierarchy is a key value
friendships are functional	friendships involve long-term loyalties or obligational commitments	friendships are restricted to one's class, caste, rank, etc.
any group is viewed as only a collection of individuals	any group is viewed as an organismic unit, inextricably interlocked	any group is viewed as a hierarchically stratified organization mapable on a genealogy or flowchart
the individual self is viewed as an entity separate from the physical world and from other persons	the individual self is viewed as organically connected with the physical world and with other persons	the individual self is viewed as hierarchically connected and appropriately located and subordinated in the physical world and with other persons
personal decisions are made by the self alone even if not in the group's best interests	personal decisions are made in consultation with the group and often in obedience or deference to its will	personal decisions are rooted in blind obedience to authority or deferential respect to tradition

(Continued)

INDIVIDUAL-CENTERED	GROUP-CENTERED	LINEAL-ORIENTED
private autonomy	corporate solidarity	linear discrimination: ethnocentrism, racism, sexism, and other "isms" based on real or imagined hierarchical ordering of values
strong personal identity	strong familial or fictive-kin identity	strong caste, class, ethnic, or other similarly lineal identity
strong desire to be personally satisfied	strong desire to be interpersonally satisfying or satisfactory	strong desire to mind one's place, honor superiors or ancestors, and to receive due respect
importance of personal time	importance of group needs	importance of tradition, the past
emotional independence from any group	emotional dependence upon the group	emotional fulfillment in the right group
involvements are calculative (individual values prevail)	involvements are moral (group values prevail)	involvements are restricted to what best serves tradition
key values are leadership and variety	key values are conformity and orderliness	key values are obedience and respect
other people are viewed in general terms (universalism)	other people are viewed in terms of competing factions, ingroups and outgroups (particularism)	other groups are viewed in terms of social status, standing, class (hierarchism)
Greater degree of social mobility	lesser to no degree of social mobility	no need for social mobility
nuclear family structure predominates	extended family or tribal structures predominate	maintaining the family line predominates

These three social patterns are available in all cultures but arranged differently by cultural preference. While the U.S. is most certainly an individualistic society for the most part, when a hardcore individualist is in an auto accident and knocked unconscious, group decisions take over: the police, the family, the medical personnel, the insurance company, and the like. On the other hand, a hale and hearty individualist who serves in the military or works in a corporation must subordinate the preferred individualist pattern to the lineal hierarchical one. The same is true in ancient Mediterranean culture which is primarily group-oriented, that is, collectivist. Everything in the middle column above describes the people we are reading about in Acts. Notice that collectivists view other people in terms of competing factions, ingroups and outgroups (particularism). This was reflected in the tension between the Hebrews and Hellenists that we just finished examining, just like between Judeans and Greeks that Paul speaks of.

Sometimes the entire collectivity or some group in the collectivity must respect hierarchical authority. A glance at the far left column in the chart above sheds further light on our reflection. The fact that the Twelve were able to address and resolve the grievance of the Hellenists about the neglect of their widows identifies and confirms this group as authoritative. Its decision is final and should be obeyed. Thus, as the hierarchical column indicates, the newly commissioned ministers have rights determined and delegated by authority. They are to behave accordingly, which they do. The preaching of Stephen and Philip are not exceptions to the ministry (which is not about waiting on tables) but sharing the wisdom that qualified them to be commissioned as ministers. Personal decisions of the newly commissioned seven are rooted in total obedience to authority. Those to whom they minister welcome and receive them with respect. The key virtues are obedience and respect.

We can mention still another characteristic of these social patterns. Collectivists are normally socialized to enjoy the duties they must fulfill, even at the cost of personal sacrifices. Individualists fulfill duties only when their calculation of advantages and disadvantages indicates a clear benefit for them. After their formal commissioning as ministers, Stephen and Philip immediately engage in their ministry with zest and intensity. Stephen loses his life, and Philip makes some interesting journeys. Yet despite the hardships and sacrifices involved in their respective ministries, each one appears to enjoy what he is doing.

The Names of the Seven

That Luke lists specific names of the Seven commissioned by the Twelve as ministers is somewhat unusual in collectivistic societies. Triandis and others point out that in collectivistic societies, the family name is more important than the given name.[8] Family is the basic group to which each person belongs, to which each person owes primary and unswerving allegiance no matter what. Hence people are identified by their family name: Pilch, John, and this is the way collectivists identify people to this day. In the ancient biblical world, this collectivist tendency to downplay the individual resulted—at least in the biblical record—in a dearth of names! In Mark's gospel, of all the people Jesus is reported to have healed, only one is named: Bar-Timaeus (Mark 10:46). That name, however, means "son of Timaeus," and identifies the father but not the healed person. So in that gospel, we know the name of no one whom Jesus healed.

Collectivist, group-oriented, ancient Mediterraneans viewed themselves in terms of genealogy (= family), gender, geography or place of origin, and the like.[9] Thus Simon, son of John (Matt 16:17), or James and John, sons of Zebedee (Luke 5:10), are examples of genealogy. Males in a family are identified by the father (Bar-Timaeus). Females are known by a male member of the family. Rebekah, daughter of Bethuel (Gen 24:24), an unmarried woman, is identified by her father. Married women are identified by reference to their husbands: Milcah, the wife of Nahor (Gen 23:15); Joanna, wife of Chuza (Luke 8:3); Priscilla, wife of Aquila (Acts 18:2). A common thread in this identification is that both men and women are identified by association with a key male: patriarch, husband.

Such identification extends even beyond the father to the clan and the ancestors of the family. John the Baptizer's father is a priest of the division of Abijah, and his mother a daughter of Aaron (Luke 1:5). Barnabas is a Levite (Acts 4:36), Paul a Benjaminite (Phil 3:5). At root, this is kinship, perhaps the most basic way that ancient Mediterraneans identified themselves.

This helps to understand identification by one's fictive family. Jesus' followers form a "household of faith" (Gal 6:10) and addressed each other as "sister" and "brother" (Mark 3:31-35; whence the title of this series of books). While the fictive group did not nature (give birth to) its members, it did nurture them, that is, provide support, concern, interest, help, and the like. This is the second most important function of a family toward its children. And just like a patriarchal family, the fictive or surrogate or substitute family (e.g., a faction, like the Twelve) has a central personage (Jesus, a father figure) whose members are like siblings. And don't they behave just like siblings? (See Luke 9:46; Mark 10:35-45).

Perhaps one last comment will sharpen our focus on the Seven. In the New Testament, we read references to a wide variety of coalitions or groups such as the Pharisees, Sadducees, Herodians, and the like. Occasionally, we even learn the name of one. For example, John 3:1 identified Nicodemus as a Pharisee. But most often, biblical authors simply identify this or that person as a Pharisee (Luke 7:36; 11:37; 18:10). Luke names only one Pharisee: Simon (7:40). The reason for this is that collectivists as a general rule tend to stereotype. If a person knows one, that person knows them all. "For Jews [Judeans] have no dealings with Samaritans" (John 4:9). "One of themselves, a prophet of their own, said, 'Cretans are always liars, evil beasts, lazy gluttons.'" (Titus 1:12). Upon hearing of Jesus of Nazareth, Nathaniel asks: "Can anything good come out of Nazareth?" (John 1:46). Nazareth, Crete, Samaria—everyone from each respective area will be the same kind of person. What difference will knowing a name make?

In his report about the tension between the Hebrews and the Hellenists, Luke refers to the Twelve as if they were a monolithic group (Acts 6:2). Later in his work, he also refers to the Hellenist group as "the Seven" (Acts 21:8), another monolithic group. Collectivists want their group to be monolithic and homogeneous with everyone thinking, feeling, and acting in the same way. This demonstrates that the group lives in harmony (Acts 4:32). Collectivists are more comfortable than individualists in the company of like-minded others. Individualists would scorn this as "group-think," but collectivists admire and desire it as a virtue.

Since this is the case with collectivists, why does Luke provide the names of the Seven? Is there any significance to the names? Before we attempt to answer these and related questions, let us review the names: Stephen, Philip, Prochorus, Nicanor, Timon, Parmenas, and Nicolaus, a proselyte of Antioch (Acts 6:5). These are all given names with no other discriminating identification such as a family name. This is strange and disconcerting to contemporary Western individualists who in many instances carry a unique social security number (which will never be recycled) to distinguish people who might by accident have identical given and family names! According to the online summary and point of access to the British Academy project, *The Lexicon of Greek Personal Names* (*LGPN*), Greeks were given only one name as indicated already in the thirteenth century BC Mycenean texts.[10] According to the project, this Indo-European pattern is found throughout most of Europe. Hence, the Hellenistic names listed by Luke may indeed be all that was known or needed to be known about these ministers.

There is also some evidence in this project of Greeks bearing two names, particularly in Asia Minor and Egypt. These names were often linked by the formula "also known as." Scholars agree that this indeed is the case for Paul: "But Saul, who is also called Paul. . ." (*Saulos de, ho kai Paulos*, Acts 13:9). The Greek adjective *saulos* means "swaggering, straddling" but connotes "loose, wanton" and was used to describe effeminate males or the style in which courtesans walked. It could be used as a nickname, but in the case of Paul and the way in which Luke presents him, *saulos* is a Greek rendition of the Hebrew *sa'ul*, which means "[the child] sought or requested from" the deity. Even so, only a very few hundred of the 215,000 individuals recorded in the *LGPN* from the Greek mainland, the Islands, and the western Mediterranean have double names. Margaret H. Williams concludes that the alternative names were often selected by reason of context specific to the person.[11]

The patronymic (father's name) was critical for identifying and legitimizing specific individuals ("Simon, son of Jonah"). But actual practice varied. And the indication of origin along with the name and patronymic depended entirely on context. In Jerusalem in the Hellenist community, the single names alone sufficed. Perhaps this explains why Nicolaus alone in the group is identified by origin: "of Antioch." Further designation that he was a proselyte reveals another important piece of information about Nicolaus. "Proselyte" is a Greek word describing a person who comes to a group from outside, a foreigner. In this sense it indicates that unlike the other six who were Jerusalemites, Nicolaus was not a native of Jerusalem/Palestine, but of Antioch (see Acts 2:10).

While some scholars claim that "proselyte" describes a "convert" to Judaism, the problem is whether it is possible for an outsider to "convert" to first-century Judaism. As Paul properly explains in Acts 13:16-43, the house of Israel consists of *descendants* of Abraham, Isaac, and Jacob, and the God of Israel was the ancestral God of Abraham, Isaac, and Jacob. People became Israelites by birth. It is impossible to "convert" to a group held together by the exclusivity deriving from common ancestry. In antiquity, ancestry-based, political-religious "conversion" was not a psychological process entailing movement from one ideology to another ideology as it is in the contemporary West. A focal feature of the Israelite ideology was requisite birth.

The Septuagint uses *proselytos* to translate the Hebrew *ger*, a resident alien or outsider who lives in an Israelite town or city.[12]

This word means "stranger, foreigner, an outsider who comes [to us]." The verb *prosêlyteuô* means to live in a place as a stranger, for example "in Israel" (Ezek 14:7). The noun *prosêlyteusis* means residence as a stranger. Thus a "proselyte" referred to an outsider who lived in an Israelite quarter of a Greco-Roman city. The "respectful" outsider (Acts 13:43) is one who showed respect for local Israelites and their traditions. They would be supportive of a forthcoming Israelite theocracy. Hence the visitors from Rome in Acts 2:10 were Judeans and outsiders resident in the Israelite section of the city. Whether these outsiders followed the customs of Judea is not specified.

In Jerusalem, Nicolaus the Antiochene is a non-Jerusalemite residing in a city with a predominantly Hebrew population. In Antioch, Nicolaus would be simply Nicolaus. The other six ministers were likely residents who had returned to Jerusalem from their place of residence elsewhere in the Hellenistic world. For these, there was no need to indicate origin.

As for the etymology of the names, Stephen (*stephanos*) means wreath or crown and indicates high status or someone held in high regard. It was a common name in the Hellenistic world.[13] Philip (*philippos*) means lover of horses, but it was also a Panhellenic name especially popular in Macedonia for the obvious reason.[14] Philip of Macedon was the father of Alexander the Great. Prochorus is a compound of *pro* + *choros* (dance, a group of dancers or singers). The name is common in later Greek. Nicanor, found in Thucydides, is also found in 1, 2, and 5 Maccabees. It seems to derive from the verb meaning conquer, prevail, vanquish.[15]

Timon appears to derive from the Greek word for honor, esteem, prestige. Parmenas (= remaining true)[16] is a short form of Parmenides (a Greek philosopher around 515 BC), Parmenion, Parmeniokos, and the like. Parmenides was a pre-Socratic philosopher admired for his exemplary life. A "Parmenidean life" was proverbial among the Greeks. Perhaps the parents who gave this name to their son intended to propose a model for his life, a goal for him to measure up to. Nicolaus, meaning victory of the people, is a compound based on the Greek word for victory (*nike*).

Simple names consist of a noun, with or without a suffix (e.g., Stephanos; Timon; Nicanor). Compound names combine nouns, adjectives, verbs, adverbs, prepositions, etc. (e.g., Philip, Prochoros, Parmenas, and Nicolaus). Compound names were often turned into endearing forms, and this might be true of these four latter ministers.

Real Names? Real People?

In a recent study, Richard Bauckham argued that the named characters in the gospel (far fewer than those unnamed) were eyewitnesses who originated the traditions associated with their names.[17] They also continued to repeat those stories as authoritative guarantors of the tradition. In view of the fact that collectivistic persons in general prefer to remain anonymous, prefer to disappear into the group, and prefer to stereotype rather than specify individuals, is this a plausible hypothesis? With regard to Stephen and the Seven, are the names authentic or did Luke borrow or create them to make an impression on the audience?

The question is hardly idle. Contributors to the *LGPN* project have tackled it head on. Simon Hornblower says historians like Herodotus and Thucydides preserved personal names to guarantee the reliability of the information given.[18] This would seem to add credibility to Bauckham's hypothesis. But what if a historian gave names to a character to provide local color or an air of authenticity? Hornblower reviews the report in Diodorus Siculus (90–21 BC) of a long speech by a certain Nicolaus (otherwise unknown to history; see Diod 13:19-28) considered by modern scholars to be a pure invention of Ephorus (400–330 BC), one of Diodorus' sources. Hornblower concludes that "the Diodoran Nicolaus of 413 BC is perhaps an example of an invented name for a fictional character, included as local color in the writings of a serious classical Greek historian."[19] Yet Hornblower adds: "A wholly invented personality, if that is what Nicolaus is, comes as a bit of a surprise in the context of the Peloponnesian War."

He argues that the names are for the most part reliable and authentic, and the *LPGN* project is gradually helping historians settle hitherto obscure questions.

Some of the data for the planned volume covering Syria and Palestine (*LGPN Part II: Commagene, Syria, Palestine, Trans-Euphratic Regions*) has already been gathered. It is, however, still not published and inaccessible. Therefore, we shall draw some tentative conclusions on the basis of what major architects and contributors to this project have supplied thus far.[20] In general, Hornblower's position deserves support. Though he favors the reliability of Greek personal names, he admits that evaluating a name requires evaluation of the author's motive. The precision with which epigraphy confirms the accuracy of personal names, as in Thucydides and others, is striking confirmation of their general accuracy and reliability. On the other hand, it is also true that authors can invent reasonable names for their historical accounts. Thus, the report that a drunken Alexander publicly kissed Bagoas the eunuch on the mouth shames and discredits Alexander whether or not Bagoas was a real person. Thus the very honorific names of the seven ministers reported by Luke certainly enhances their status even if the names were not their authentic names. This would fit the tendency in antiquity to name the nameless with the passage of time.[21]

Conclusion

In sum, Stephen and all the Seven are true to type as collectivistic persons. They care about their Hellenistic ingroup. They complain that the Hebrews are slighting their widows. Conflict in Israel between ingroup and outgroup within the house of Israel has a long history in the Israelite tradition. The Samaritan offer to assist the returned exiles and new Persian colonists in Yehud in rebuilding the temple was rebuffed (Ezra 4:1-3). While some Samaritans and some returned exiles had once been part of an ingroup, at this point in history a different ingroup-outgroup configuration exists. By giving honorific names (whether authentic or fictional) to seven key males in the Hellenistic out-group in Jerusalem, Luke further enhances the newly elevated status of the Seven to which we now turn our attention.

CHAPTER 3

Stephen, a Minister (not a Deacon!)

In the Introduction, we noted that Pope Benedict XVI said that Stephen and his companions were not deacons! He correctly reminded his audience that that Greek word *diakonos* is never used in Acts. The office and function of "deacons" are later historical developments. In Roman Catholicism, the restoration of the "permanent diaconate" requested by the Second Vatican Council (*Lumen Gentium*, no. 29) was implemented by Pope Paul VI in his *Motu Proprio "Sacrum diaconatus ordinem,"* promulgated on the feast of St. Ephraem the Syrian, deacon and Doctor of the Church, June 18, 1967. The American bishops were granted their request to ordain celibate and married men permanently to the diaconate in April 1968. The first permanent deacons in the U.S. were ordained in 1971. Still it should be noted that contemporary permanent deacons and their functions are dramatically different from deacons in the earliest times. One major difference is that contemporary permanent deacons are clergy. Deacons in the biblical period were not. Stephen and his companions were neither deacons nor clergy.

Origins of Deacons

Well, then, who were the Seven in Acts of the Apostles? More specifically, what was their status and role? To answer this question we will reflect on the Greek word *diakonos* (defined by Frederick Danker as "one who serves as an intermediary in a transaction, an agent, an intermediary, a broker")[1] and associated Greek words: *diakonein* ("to function as an intermediary, a go-between, a broker") and *diakonia* ("service especially rendered in an intermediary capacity"). In the terminology of linguistics, the English word, "deacon," is a loanword. This means it is essentially a transliteration of the Greek from which it is derived. Loanwords are also at least partially "naturalized" in the new language into which they have been integrated. The English word "deacon" carries many meanings today that its Greek counterpart did not. In general, "deacon" today describes a holder of an office in the ministry. Deacons (and sometimes deaconesses) exist in Roman Catholicism, the Church of England, Lutheranism, Presbyterianism, and Baptist and Congregational churches among others, but their ministerial role and functions differ. However, it is clear that there is no specific connection between deacons of contemporary times and deacons in antiquity. There certainly is no connection between either deacons (contemporary or ancient) and the Seven who were appointed in Acts 6.[2] For this reason, we will not use the English word "deacon," because its contemporary meaning is irrelevant to the past and would cause unnecessary confusion.

Brief Historical Sketch of *Diakonos*

In what follows, I rely heavily on the major critical study of this and related words and concepts conducted and published by John N. Collins.[3] The noun *diakonos* appears just six times in the Septuagint, the Greek translation of the Old Testament (Esth 1:10; 2:2; 6:3, 5; Prov 10:4, a verse not in the Hebrew Bible; and

4 Macc 9:17). The New Testament writers used that common noun (*diakonos*) and its related abstract noun (*diakonia*) and verb (*diakonein*) much more often. In Paul's letters, the earliest New Testament documents (AD 49–63), *diakonos* designates a servant (and *diakonia*, service), and often it is a nonspecific title designating a servant of or intermediary between Messiah-Jesus and God and other human beings. Paul sent Timothy to the Thessalonians and described him as "our brother and God's servant [*diakonos*] in the gospel of Christ" (1 Thess 3:2). Speaking of himself to the Corinthians, Paul says: "We put no obstacle in any one's way, so that no fault may be found with our ministry [*diakonia*, service], but as servants [*diakonoi*] of God we commend ourselves in every way" (2 Cor 6:3-4). Jesus commends the Twelve to be servants and serve others: "If any one would be first, he must be last of all and servant [*diakonos*] of all" (Mark 9:35). The context of this same saying in Matthew 20:26-28 further nuances the idea. "It shall not be so among you; but whoever would be great among you must be your servant [*diakonos*], and whoever would be first among you must be your slave [*doulos*]; even as the Son of man came not to be served [*diakonethenai*] but to serve [*diakonesai*], and to give his life as a ransom for many."

In two of Paul's letters, however, the word *diakonos* seems to identify some sort of position or status in a local church, but the precise meaning is not clear. "Paul and Timothy, servants [*douloi*] of Christ [Messiah] Jesus, to all the saints in Christ [Messiah] Jesus who are at Philippi, with the bishops [overseers] and deacons [*diakonoi*]" (Phil 1:1). And again, "I commend to you our sister Phoebe, a deaconess [*diakonos*, the Greek word has no feminine form] of the church at Cenchreae" (Rom 16:1). In Philippi the *diakonoi* are associated with the overseers (often translated anachronistically as bishops). The overall sense of these two references from Paul's letters is that the *diakonoi* (which included women) assisted church leaders and may even, as Phoebe, have served as a communication link between congregations.

Late in the first century AD the word *diakonos* begins to acquire a more specific meaning of services or ministries distinctive to

the Messianist community, but still in a very general and diversi-
fied sense. In Acts 6:1 we read of one kind of *diakonia* among the
Hellenists and Hebrews, while in Acts 6:4 the Twelve dedicate
themselves to another kind of *diakonia*. We will examine this case
more closely after we complete this brief historical sketch of the
origins of the *diakonos*.

In the Pastoral letters (ca. AD 100), there is clear evidence of
a more developed church order, at least in the Aegean area
(Titus) and Asia Minor (Timothy). Rules for appointing overseers
(it is probably legitimate to begin using the word "bishop" at
this point) and *diakonoi* are presented in 1 Tim 3:1-13. What is
clear in this passage is that *diakonoi* are in the service of the
overseer (bishop). Thus it is reasonable to conclude that the term
diakonos in Philippians 1:1; Romans 16:1; and 1 Timothy 3:8 is
already a technical term. Further clarification and specification
of the duties of a *diakonos* begin to emerge in various post-biblical
documents with more frequency from this point on.

In his First Epistle to the Corinthians 42.4, Clement of Rome
(ca. AD 96) describes the order of ministers in the church. God
sent Jesus who in turn sent apostles to preach the imminence of
theocracy. The apostles in their turn appointed overseers and
diakonoi ("bishops and deacons of future believers") in imitation
and fulfillment of Isaiah 60:17 (in the Septuagint). Deacons here
are liturgical assistants, or ritual waiters at the sacred meal. Ignatius of Antioch (ca. AD 110) makes this interesting observation
about deacons: "It behooves you also, in every way, to please the
deacons, who are [ministers] of the mysteries of Christ Jesus; for
they are not ministers of meat and drink, but servants of the
Church of God" (Epistle to the Trallians 2). Ignatius thus indicates
that deacons are significant as "godly officers" of the bishop rather
than for their role at a table. It will be well to remember this later
when we examine the role of *diakonoi* waiting at tables.

In the *Apostolic Tradition of Hippolytus of Rome* (ca. AD 215; 8:2),
the *diakonos* is ordained to the service of the bishop especially
in eucharistic and baptismal liturgies. This was a significant shift
from service to the community, the circumstance in which the

diakonoi originated. The laying on of hands in this ceremony marks an initiation into an "order," and this is how *diakonoi* came to be regarded as clergy.

With the influx of catechumens into the church after Constantine, *diakonoi* were enlisted to instruct these newcomers in the faith. Some administered smaller churches in the bishop's name, but the bishop presided over liturgies and initiated new Christians. As presbyters gained in importance, the role of *diakonoi* diminished. With the approach of the fifth century AD, the *diakonos* was viewed as a step toward the presbyterate. By the end of this century, it all but vanished. The discussion that has preceded and which will now follow are heavily indebted to John N. Collins[4] whose opinions are reflected in nearly all contemporary discussion of *diakonia* (ministry).

Acts 6:1-6 (RSV)

Now in these days when the disciples were increasing in number, the Hellenists murmured against the Hebrews because their widows were neglected in the daily distribution [*diakonia*]. And the twelve summoned the body of the disciples and said, "It is not right that we should give up preaching the word of God to serve [*diakonein*] tables. Therefore, brethren, pick out from among you seven men of good repute, full of the Spirit and of wisdom, whom we may appoint to this duty. But we will devote ourselves to prayer and to the ministry [*diakonia*] of the word." And what they said pleased the whole multitude, and they chose Stephen, a man full of faith and of the Holy Spirit, and Philip, and Prochorus, and Nicanor, and Timon, and Parmenas, and Nicolaus, a proselyte of Antioch.

We have inserted into this translation those places where the Greek noun *diakonia* and verb *diakonein* appear. Thus, the segment deals with service or ministry, but it does not identify anyone involved as a *diakonos*. How did the word *diakonos* come to be associated with Stephen and the Seven? The first reference seems to be in a work by Irenaeus of Lyon (d. 202), *Adversus Haereses (Against Heresies)* III.10: "And still further, Stephen, who was chosen the first deacon by the apostles, and who, of all men, was the first to follow the footsteps of the martyrdom of the Lord, being the first that was slain for confessing Christ, speaking boldly among the people, and teaching . . ." Though originally written in Greek, this work survived only in a Latin translation. The word "deacon" in Irenaeus' statement was transliterated into Latin as *diaconos* from the Greek *diakonos*. The problem, of course, is that Luke did not use that word in Acts. Irenaeus' presentation of Stephen as the biblical model for the office of deacon as he might have known it in his day was repeated in later texts alongside the image of the servanthood of Jesus (Matt 20:28).

What, then, did Luke report? A comparison of Luke with Paul indicates that they nuance the abstract noun (*diakonia*) and the verb (*diakonein*) in a similar way. This usage can be illustrated schematically:

Greek:	Luke	Paul
diakonein (vb): associated with coworkers in mission	Acts 19:22: Timothy and Erastus (two "helpers" to or coworkers with Paul)	Phlm 13: Onesimus, on behalf of Philemon, "serves" Paul imprisoned for the gospel
diakonia (abstract noun): a) describing apostolic commission	Acts 1:17, 25: this "ministry": v. 17, Judas; v. 25 Matthias Acts 20:25: Paul: the "ministry" I received.	Rom 11:13: magnify my "ministry" to Israelite minorities in non-Israelite majorities (my interpretation[5])

(Continued)

Greek:	Luke	Paul
diakonia b) of mediating divine revelation	Acts 6:4: the Twelve and "ministry" of the word; 21:19: Paul's "ministry" among Israelite minorities	2 Cor 4:1: "ministry" Paul referring back to 3:16, 18; 2 Cor 5:18: Paul's "ministry" of reconciliation; 2 Cor 6:3: "ministry" referring back to 6:1
diakonia c) of delegations between churches	Acts 11:29: to send help from Antioch to Jerusalem according to "ability"; Acts 12:25: Paul and Barnabas return from Antioch to Jerusalem having finished their "mission"	Rom 15:31: Paul's "service" to Jerusalem; 2 Cor 8:4: Macedonians sent "relief" to Jerusalem; 9:1: "offering" for the saints (in Jerusalem); 9:13: test of this "service" (to send "relief")

In columns 2 and 3 where I have reported the RSV text, I have placed in quotation marks the English word that is rendering the Greek word in column 1. Readers who don't read or understand Greek ought not despair over the diversity of English words in their translations. They should rather grind their teeth (Acts 7:54) against translators who are trying to do them a favor. Bad enough that Ignatius set the Acts 6 segment down a path of misunderstanding. Translators only compound the problem. As the Italian proverb puts it, "every translator is a traitor." Even though it is heavily freighted in contemporary church-speak, the word "ministry" is the most appropriate translation of *diakonia*, but it must be used with caution and be stripped of its contemporary significance. For the most part, modern "ministers" tend to freely assign this term to whatever it is they do for the believing community. Ushers, greeters, those who serve coffee after liturgy, and the like all call themselves "ministers." There is no support for this practice in the Bible or in ecclesial documents.

What is of greater significance for our discussion is that Luke does not use the common noun, *diakonos*, either in his gospel or in Acts! Collins[6] thinks this is because Luke was convinced that the connotations of that word even then were inappropriate for expressing his understanding of the message of the gospel. What then is Luke saying in his report?

To begin with, a close reading of Acts of the Apostles reveals that *diakonia* is a major interest of and concern for Luke. At the beginning of Acts (1:8), the Lord Jesus commissions the Eleven to be his witnesses in Jerusalem and from there to the end of the earth. Peter then inducts Matthias into their *diakonia* (Acts 1:17, 25). There are some key points to notice in this report. A candidate for *diakonia* is recommended by the entire community (120 people here, Acts 1:15). The candidate, further, must be qualified: "one of the men who have accompanied us during all the time that the Lord Jesus went in and out among us, beginning from the baptism of John until the day when he was taken up from us" to become "with us a witness to his resurrection" (Acts 1:21-22). These credentials must be verified.

The community put forward two qualified candidates: Joseph called Barsabbas, surnamed Justus, and Matthias (Acts 1:23). Then the community prayed (Acts 1:24) and made its selection by casting lots (Acts 1:26). Since God determines how lots will turn out, the actual selection is by God. Thus in Luke's understanding the community identifies ministers and God authenticates ministry.

Toward the end of Acts as Paul concludes his journeys, he addresses the elders of the community at Miletus and expresses the hope that "I may accomplish my course and the ministry [*diakonia*] which I received from the Lord Jesus, to testify to the gospel of the grace of God" (Acts 20:24). Paul was inducted into and authenticated for *diakonia* by God through Jesus (Acts 9:15).

Shortly afterward in Jerusalem, Paul reports to James and all the elders what God had done among Israelite minorities living among non-Israelites through his *diakonia* (Acts 21:19). Thus the concept of *diakonia* serves as an inclusio for Luke; it is one concept among others that signals the beginning and end of his report. Keeping this in mind will guide our investigation of *diakonia* in Acts 6.

The Problem

One problem that arose in Jerusalem between Hellenists and Hebrews was a grievance that the Hellenist widows were being neglected in the daily *diakonia* (Acts 6:1). The Twelve replied that "it is not right" to give up preaching the word of God in order to *diakonein* tables (tables in the dative case; Acts 6:2). In the schematic outline of Greek words above, it would seem that none of the meanings of *diakonia* would suit verse 1. Translators reflect puzzlement and impose unwarranted interpretations on these words. Their renditions of *diakonia* include the following: "ministration" (KJV; Rheims: "the act of ministering"); "daily distribution" (RSV; NEB; JB; NJB; NAB revised NT 1986); "daily distribution of food" (NAB 1970; NRSV; NIV; Goodspeed); "daily distribution of funds" (GN); and "when the food supplies were given out each day" (CEV).

According to Collins,[7] "distribution" is an entirely inappropriate term whether it refer to food or money. Linguistically, distribution is not one of the attested meanings of *diakonia*. In this context, the idea of *diakonia* is that the widows are indeed not being provisioned, so *diakonia* means attending to people (not tables; see Plutarch, *Moralia* 174d), or making arrangements for such attention (Josephus, *Ant* 8.169), or even engaging in such ministration (ministry, service) as a ritual (*Test. Job* 11:2; 15:1). The Hebrew Twelve are not attending to the Hellenistic widows.

The verb (*diakonein*) in Acts 6:2 is similarly misinterpreted. Because this verb is followed by a Greek word meaning table (in the dative case), that noun appears to control the way translators gloss the verb. Renditions include: "serve tables" (KJV; Rheims; RSV); "serve at table" (NAB revised NT 1986); "wait at table" (NEB); "wait at tables" (NRSV); "wait on tables" (NAB 1970; NIV); "Give out food" (JB; NJB); "handle finances (GN); " keep accounts" (Goodspeed); "serve at tables" (CEV). In a note to verse 2 concerning the activity of the Twelve at tables, the CEV explains: "This may mean either that they were in charge of handing out food to the widows or that they were in charge of the money, since the Greek word 'table' may also mean 'bank.'" Collins shows how a similar phrase in the *Testament of Job* (12:2): "to attend on the poor at table" recommends precisely such a translation for Acts 6:2. Focus is on the people, not the tables. In fact, in the wider evidence of Greek literature, tables are rarely mentioned because the nuance of *diakonia* means to get something for someone, or bring something to someone as the verse in *Testament of Job* plainly states. *Diakonia* means tending to, caring for, paying attention to. The economic translations in CEV, GN, and Goodspeed have no foundation in Greek literature at all. Luke knows how to report financial transactions. The Apostles squat, people put donations at their feet, and they redistribute the funds (see Acts 4:35). Clearly, that is not what Luke intends to express here in Acts 6.

Collins argues further that the dative case used with the verb *diakonein* quite likely indicates the service has nothing at all to do with tables. What is at stake is the service or ministry itself. Reviewing what has taken place in the first five chapters of Acts helps a reader to understand the problem with greater clarity. From the beginning of Acts, the Twelve are engaged in preaching and teaching in the temple and in homes (Acts 2:44-47; 5:42). They also address basic human material needs (4:32-35). What's wrong with this picture? The Hebrew Twelve speak Aramaic (see Acts 2:7); the Hellenist widows don't understand Aramaic. They are not likely to go to the temple where the Aramaic language prevails. Neither would they feel comfortable in the homes of Aramaic speaking believers where the conversation and teaching would be in the same language. The Hellenist widows are missing out on the teaching to which every believer has a right!

The topic of concern here, therefore, is the public and perhaps even ritual performance of a specific set of duties in the community, a ministry, for Hellenist widows who were being neglected by the Hebrew Twelve to the dismay of the Hellenists. The matter is serious and engages the Twelve with the same urgency as their perceived need to replace Judas in their *diakonia* (Acts 1:17, 26). The solemn use of this word, *diakonia*, in selecting a replacement for Judas recurs here in Acts 6:4 where the Twelve recommit themselves to prayer and the *diakonia* of the word. The solemnity is underscored by Luke with the phrase used by the Twelve to indicate how they decided to resolve this crisis in ministry: "It is not right. . ." (6:2). In the Septuagint this complete phrase is commonly reported thus: "It is not right in the sight of God. . ." (see Deut 6:18; 12:25; 13:18; Exod 15:26). This is not God's will.

Since the Twelve are the only ones thus far in the Acts story line who have been instituted in a ministry (*diakonia*) and this by the Lord Jesus personally, they are embarking on a new venture in Acts 6. They are about to institute the very first community-determined ministry. That is the force of the word "duty" (Acts 6:3: *chreia*, office, duty, service, something that is needed). Notice, however, that they do not specify where this duty is to be exercised, whether where people eat or where they receive financial assistance. Subsequent teaching and preaching activity by two of the Seven, Stephen and Philip, are thus not exceptions but rather the expected exercise of this ministry; it is their assigned duty.

A Commissioned Role

Perhaps the most significant contribution by Collins to a fresh understanding of *diakonia*, ministry, was captured in the title of the book that offered a simplified presentation and further development of his research: *Are all Christians Ministers?* His answer was a resounding no! In the aftermath of the Second Vatican Council, perhaps especially its Decree on the Apostolate of the Laity (*Apostolicam Actuositatem*, which reserved the word "ministry" for the clergy!), the word "ministry" began to proliferate in church life like mushrooms after the rain. Many of these ministries were self-declared. Collins' critique of trends in the theology of ministry at the time of his writing (1990–92) was timely and is still valid. The significance of Collins' research for our purposes is at least twofold. One, he provides the evidence that the role of deacon did not emerge in Acts of the Apostles, not even in the story of the Seven (Acts 6). Two, what Luke has recorded in Acts 6 is the formal institution of a ministry as a commissioned role. That is why Collins' answer to the question: Are all Christians ministers? is No! Commissioning determines a ministry. To this we now turn closer attention.

Just as with the selection of Matthias to replace Judas, so too here the Twelve instruct the Hellenist community to select seven qualified men to address this need. It should be recalled that scholars are agreed that a Hebrew/Hellenist division already existed in the Israelite community at least from the time of Alexander the Great. Scholars also assume that each group took care of its needs, whether teaching or social care. The decision of the Twelve to select seven men for a specific duty is not the innovation. What is new is that they will be authenticated to fulfill a determined service. The community is the agency that identifies and selects seven candidates for *diakonia*, just as the 120 proposed two candidates to replace Judas in the *diakonia* of the Twelve.

The Twelve also specify the credentials these male candidates must possess: they must be of good repute, filled with the Spirit, and wise. (While there is evidence for female deacons among the early believers, e.g., Rom 16:1, in this instance Luke uses the Greek word that identifies males alone.) Good repute is essential in honor-based cultures such as the ancient Middle East. These candidates must be able to make a public claim to sterling reputation, honor, and good-standing that will be accepted, respected, and confirmed by the public. There can be no skeletons in the closet. There can be no risk that anyone in the community might challenge the claim to good repute and thus shame the nominated candidate, or worse yet, the commissioned candidate at a later time.

A person "full of the Spirit" would be identified in this culture as a holy person.[8] Such a person is one who has ready access to the spirit world where God and spirits reside, and one who is able to broker favors from that world to human beings. In this regard, a holy person often has one or more special helping spirits for assistance and protection. In the garden, an angel ministered to Jesus (Luke 22:43). A holy person has control over spirits and not vice versa (Luke 4:39 where Jesus rebukes and expels the spirit "fever"[9]). The vehicle by which a holy person makes contact with the spirit world (or vice versa) is an ASC, a level of awareness other than the ordinary (1 Sam 3:1; more than twenty references to this in Acts including Stephen in Acts 7:55-56). The holy person uses divine gifts for the benefit of others rather than for self-aggrandizement (e.g., Acts 8:9-13, 18-24). One of the major gifts brokered from the spirit world to human beings is healing (Acts 3:1-10).

The third requirement is wisdom. This could have many wide-ranging meanings, but in view of the fact that two of the Seven, Stephen and Philip, go on to "preach," wisdom surely entails a knowledge of the sacred traditions, the Greek Scriptures (the Septuagint), especially as they help to understand Jesus. In other words, these candidates for *diakonia* are going to be authenticated as preachers. They must be honorable men, intimately familiar with God, and knowledgeable in the Septuagint especially as it can help other Hellenists to accept Jesus raised by God from the dead, Messiah and Cosmic Lord soon to inaugurate theocracy. Since the context here is Hellenist widows who cannot understand the Aramaic preaching of the Twelve, the task will be to instruct these widows and other believers in the Greek language for a deeper appreciation of the faith.

Once such candidates have been identified and their credentials validated (a process missing in Luke's highly condensed and very high-context report), the Twelve appoint them to their new duties (*chreia*). The ritual involves prayer and laying hands on the approved candidates. These new ministers differ from the Twelve in one very significant way: no one among the Seven accompanied Jesus from his Baptism until his Ascension. They are not eyewitnesses. Thus a different sent of credentials were required for this new ministry.

Conclusion

Stephen was one of the Seven who were inducted by the Twelve into a commissioned ministry or service. The Seven were not called deacons by Luke nor were they deacons in fact. Their ministry was created specifically to address the needs of Hellenist widows, but from their subsequent activity we see that these newly commissioned ministers taught and preached (among Hellenists) in Israel and beyond (Acts 7:2-53; 11:19). According to Luke's report, Stephen is the community's first choice. The community recognized Stephen as "a man full of faith and of the Holy Spirit " (Acts 6:5). Faith as a Middle Eastern value is loyalty.[10] Stephen is a believer totally faithful to God. Spirit in Middle Eastern cultural perspective is power, and the Holy Spirit is specifically the power of God. Because Stephen, the holy man, is totally loyal to God, God freely gives him a share in divine power.

Luke reports immediate confirmation of Stephen's ministerial credentials. Stephen, "full of grace [= God's favor] and power [= a share in God's omnipotence], did great wonders and signs among the people" (Acts 6:8). Though none are specified, the phrase "wonders and signs" is borrowed from the Septuagint's description of God's mighty deeds on behalf of Israel (e.g., Exod 7:3; Deut 4:34; 28:46; 29:2; 34:11; Ps 135:9; Isa 8:18). Stephen makes one such reference in his speech (Acts 7:36), but Luke uses the phrase often in Acts (2:43; 4:30; 5:12; 6:8; 7:36; 14:3; and 15:12).

As a holy man, Stephen had direct contact with God who empowered him to act on the divine behalf and broker healing favors from God to needy human beings. Even before his speech, his opponents "could not withstand the wisdom and the Spirit with which he spoke" (Acts 6:10). The speech (Acts 7:2-53), of course, is the crowning testimony by which Stephen proves himself to be exactly the kind of minister that the community identified and credentialed and the Twelve inducted into this new ministry (*diakonia*).

CHAPTER 4

Stephen, a Holy Man and His Vision(s)

I n chapter 3 we noted that one necessary qualification in order to be a candidate for ministry was to be "full of the Spirit," that is, a holy person. This is a long-standing exhortation in the Israelite tradition: "Say to all the congregation of the people of Israel, You shall be holy; for I the LORD your God am holy" (Lev 19:2). Every Israelite was expected to be holy, that is, set apart, special to the Lord, therefore different from "them." The Holiness Code (Lev 17–26) explained how to be holy. In general, it pointed out things Israelites ("we") ought to do. The prohibitions referred to what "they" (the outsiders) did. "We" should not behave like "them."

This raises an interesting point about Stephen and his companions. As Hellenists, they sometimes were in no position to keep the Holiness Code with all its requirements. Recall what we said about Hellenists in chapter 1. Yet the Hellenist community certified that the Seven were indeed "full of the Spirit," or holy persons. The Twelve accepted and confirmed this decision. Thus, it would seem that at this time there existed at least two ways to be considered a spirit-filled person, a holy person. The Hebrews took a narrow, conservative view, quite appropriate for someone living in Israel. The Hellenists took a broader, more adaptive view, quite necessary living outside of Israel. The entire "house of Israel" recognized that there were many ways to please God, to be holy (i.e., set apart for God).

As noted earlier, all cultures recognize a holy person, that is, someone who has privileged and facile access to the spirit realm and who can broker favors from that realm to needy human beings. Anthropologists have identified such a person among the Siberian Tungus who is called a shaman. Some anthropologists and other scholars have applied this term to holy persons in other cultures. I prefer to use the word that the culture itself uses. In Israel, such a person was a *ṣaddiq* or *ḥasid*. While the *ṣaddiq* fulfilled the essential requirements of holiness, the *ḥasid* went over and beyond to remove any doubt about pleasing God. It is noteworthy that in the Markan story line, this is the very first title and status ascribed to Jesus by an unclean spirit: " I know who you are, the Holy One of God" (Mark 1:24).

Stephen and His Companions: Holy Persons

In a previous publication,[1] I presented a model of the characteristics of a holy person (shaman) across cultures drawn up by anthropologist Joan Townsend. Then, in accord with the social science method of interpreting the Bible, I modified and applied this model to the Synoptics. Here I apply that modified model to Stephen and his companions.

1. A holy person makes direct experiential contact or has direct communication with spirits. In general, across cultures spirits can be sentient beings (animal or humanlike spirits), forces of nature (Jesus calms the wind which word in Hebrew can signify wind, breath, and spirit), or transcendent energy. A holy person will usually have one or more special helping spirits for assistance and protection. Later Christian

tradition spoke of "guardian angels." At the end of his speech, Stephen gazed into the sky and saw God and Jesus at the right hand. Clearly Stephen had direct experiential contact with the divine realm.

2. A holy person controls the spirits and not vice versa. Luke tells us that Stephen, "full of grace and power, did great wonders and signs" (Acts 6:8). The wonders and signs quite likely included exorcisms, which would testify to Stephen's (and his companions') ability to control spirits and not fall victim to them.

3. The holy person also controls the alternate state of consciousness (ASC) or level of awareness at which he makes contact with the spirit world. True, if a spirit is unwilling, there will be no contact. But ethnographic data indicates that controlling the imagery of one's ASC is a key element of a holy man's technique. All visionaries control the imagery of their trance. "At least in some measure, people see what they expect to see."[2] Thus, while Luke reports only this single ASC experience by Stephen, it is one of more than twenty that he records in Acts. So it is reasonable to conclude that Stephen has had other similar experiences. In this instance (Acts 7:53-54), Stephen has an ASC experience and describes it to his audience. Only the visionary can interpret the vision, and Stephen does so immediately with ease and assurance. In fact, in this entire final scenario of the conclusion of his speech and his murder, Luke presents Stephen as a person quite in charge of his condition.

Experts have identified more than thirty-five different levels of awareness.[3] Some examples are dreaming, sleeping, hypnagogic (drowsiness before sleep), hypnopompic (semi-consciousness preceding waking), hyperalert, lethargic, rapture, hysteric, fragmentation, regressive, meditative, trance, reverie, daydreaming, internal scanning, stupor, coma, stored memory, expanded consciousness, and "normal" among others. In many of these states, a person is able to control the imagery.

4. The ASC experience of a holy person manifests a "this worldly" focus on the material world. Two chief results of ASC experiences are the discovery of a solution to a problem or revelation of a new direction one ought to take in life. Both results relate to the here and now of the visionary. Either one of these would well describe what Stephen experienced. The vision of God and Jesus in the sky, in alternate reality, assures him that he was right in his preaching, and his accusers were wrong. Caught in a hopeless situation (about to lose his life), he nevertheless is confident that he is headed toward his reward for loyalty. He will soon enter the spirit realm and join the company of God and Jesus. This surely strengthened him to endure what was about to happen.

Further, a holy person uses his or her abilities for the benefit of individuals or the community and not for personal aggrandizement in any way. Stephen's communication of his vision to those present may have had an impact on Paul in the audience. Of course, this was not directly intended by Stephen, but his report heard by all may have affected more than Paul. This experience stands in contrast to what Simon Magus envisioned for himself if Peter would share that divine gift with him (Acts 8:9-13, 18-24).

5. Holy persons travel to and through the spirit world by taking "sky journeys" (called "soul flight" in anthropological literature). The holy person can travel in the spirit world while both feet are planted solidly on the ground. Often a protective spirit or "familiar" helps in this journey. Similar events would include out-of-the-body experiences (OOBEs), "astral projection," and near death or clinical death experiences. The astral prophet John who recorded the content of his ASC experiences in the book of Revelation (Rev 1:10) explicitly admits he took such journeys (Rev 4:2; 17:3; 21:20). At this point in his life, Stephen has not taken a journey to the sky. He stands solidly on the ground as he gazes up into

the sky. However, given his familiarity with what he sees, one can conjecture that he has visited that place before.

These five characteristics are central to the identity and function of a holy person. There are three others which are related.

6. In the encounter with spirits, the holy person can interact without fear of them possessing him. In some cultures, holy persons do become possessed by spirits, but this does not seem to be the case in biblical culture. Successful in his "great wonders and signs," Stephen does not seem to have been harmed by pernicious spirits.

7. The holy person remembers at least some aspects of the ASC. The prophets are continually reminded to "write this down" or "write the vision down" (e.g., Jer 30:2; 36:2, 28; Hab 2:2). At this point in his life, Stephen has no time for recording his experience. On the other hand, whether Luke reports a factual element or has contrived this part of his report, the point is that Stephen immediately tells what he has seen. In reports of such experiences, visionaries admit that this sometimes occurs, though more often the full recollection and interpretation of an experience comes after a (long) period of reflection.[4]

8. Healing is a major focus of a holy person's activity. One of the characteristics of a person entering an ASC is that her/ his looking becomes fixed as if in a "gaze" or a "stare." This verb occurs in such contexts in Acts of the Apostles (Acts 1:10; 7:55; 10:4; 11:6). When used in the context of healing, it is plausible to conclude that a person with healing ability induces a trance for the express purpose of healing (Peter in Acts 3:4; Paul in Acts 14:9). Stephen's "great wonders and signs" may have included healing events, though nothing specific is mentioned. If so, they may very well have been effected in an ASC as Luke records about others elsewhere in Acts.

The Call of Stephen and His Companions
to be Holy Persons

In *Lumen Gentium*, the Second Vatican Council's Dogmatic
Constitution on the Church, chapter 5 describes "The Call of the
Whole Church to Holiness." This chapter represents nearly two
thousand years of reflection on and working out of God's injunc-
tion in Leviticus 19:2: "You shall be holy; for I the LORD your
God am holy" (Lev 19:2). In the Israelite tradition, the call to be
a holy person was universal. The Scriptures and subsequent
tradition record, however, that many refused to heed the call.
The rabbinic sources variously report that the Messiah will come
when Israel has repented a single day; or when all Israel observed a single Sabbath properly; when Israel observed two
Sabbaths in a row properly; and many similar reasons. What
these opinions share in common is that all Israel has not responded to the universal call to holiness.

Some few, however, have responded to the call with total
loyalty. The writing prophets are prime examples. How does
the call to be a holy person come? And how is a candidate initiated into that status? On a previous occasion in Tutzing, Ger-
many, I adopted an anthropological model describing this
process across cultures and applied it to Jesus.[5] Here I return to
that model and apply it to Stephen and his companions. Anthropologists identify six elements in the call and initiation.

1. The spirit contacts the holy person with the intention of
   adopting or possessing him. (The notion of possession here
   is "positive," that is, the spirit elects to use this human person for good deeds. In some cultures, possession is viewed
   as "negative," that is, the spirit intends to harm or destroy
   this person.) Luke describes Stephen as "enspirited" or filled
   with (possessed by) the spirit: Acts 6:5, 7 ("full of power");
   7:55.

2. The adopting or possessing spirit identifies itself. Since
   Stephen recognizes the beings he is seeing in the sky at the

end of his speech (Acts 7:55-56), the spirits have obviously revealed themselves to him on earlier occasions in his life.

3. The holy person needs to acquire basic, necessary ritual skills. The word "ritual" is important because anthropological data and statistical research indicate that the overwhelming majority of societies engage in trance behavior during religious rituals. Thus, holy persons should be the most adept at this behavior in the context of religious ritual, which means they would need to learn and hone basic ritual skills. These skills would include strategies for inducing religious ecstatic trance as well as additional skills requisite during the trance. Stephen's vision at the end of his speech, and his success in performing "great wonders and signs among the people" (Acts 6:8) confirm that he indeed learned the basic necessary skills of a holy man: how to induce trance, and how to broker healing from the spirit world.

One key linguistic indication of trance in Luke is the Greek verb translated "gaze." This word appears just fourteen times in the New Testament. Paul uses it twice (2 Cor 3:7, 13), but Luke uses it twelve times and of these, ten occur in Acts: 1:10; 3:4, 12; 6:15; 7:55; 10:4; 11:6; 13:9; 14:9; 23:1; see also Luke 4:20; 22:56. Malina and Pilch observe that this verb belongs to the vocabulary of holy man procedures and ASC behavior.[6] Specific instances are reported in Acts 1:10 (the Eleven); 3:4 (Peter along with John); 7:55 (Stephen); 10:4 (Peter); 11:6 (Peter); 13:9 and 14:9 (Paul healing). The verb does not have this ASC connotation in Acts 3:12; 6:15; 23:1.

What are the circumstances in which this verb suggests a holy man or ASC context? First, the subject is a holy person, that is a *ṣaddiq* or *ḥasid*.[7] God customarily communicates with holy persons in an ASC (1 Sam 3:1). Passages containing the verb "stare" pointing to an ASC thus indicate the subject is a holy man (Acts 3:4, Peter; 7:55, Stephen, etc.). As such, the subject would be expected to have direct access to God and the ability to broker favors from God to other human beings. This is indeed the case in these passages.

Second, the subject of this verb is at prayer or in trance. Since Peter and John were going specifically to the temple for the three o'clock hour of prayer (Acts 3:1), they could already have been praying as they walked. It is not unusual among modern Jews, especially in the Conservative and Orthodox traditions, to pray in the synagogue, turn to greet or converse with others, and return to prayer. The activity is seamless.

But an equally plausible explanation is that a holy man induces a trance when conditions are right for it. This is easily accomplished especially in a culture where altering states of consciousness intentionally or unintentionally is second nature. One is enculturated in the technique and appropriate rite. All the more so a holy man. Indeed, gazing or staring or looking intently (as in other instances in Acts) might not only be the sign of being in trance but also a technique for inducing trance, a part of the requisite rite. Think of daydreaming with eyes wide open. From the perspective of cognitive neuroscience, such intense concentration can induce a trance "from the top down." This level of consciousness originates primarily in the brain, either by clearing the mind of all thoughts or focusing intensely on a thought, and then engages the entire body.

In Acts 6:15 when Stephen is hailed before the Sanhedrin and put on trial, he knew what awaited him. He remembered Jesus' promise: "But before all this they will lay their hands on you and persecute you, delivering you up to the synagogues and prisons, and you will be brought before kings and governors for my name's sake. This will be a time for you to bear testimony. Settle it therefore in your minds, not to meditate beforehand how to answer; for I will give you a mouth and wisdom, which none of your adversaries will be able to withstand or contradict" (Luke 21:12-15). Focusing intently on Jesus' promise and on the defense he is expected to make before the Sanhedrin, Stephen very plausibly induced a trance. Intense concentration can trigger a trance.

That the council members observed "his face was like the face of an angel" (Acts 6:15) suggests they observed one possible result of entering trance: a physical metamorphosis visible to others.

Third, the visionary communicates extraordinary intuition, wisdom. That the speech of Stephen (possibly) delivered in trance (Acts 7:2-53) is filled with remarkable on-the-spot wisdom (even if it is a Lukan composition) should not be a surprise. All of his preaching was full of irrefutable wisdom which his opponents could not withstand (Acts 6:10). Since some of this preaching may not have taken place in trance, one can imagine the heightened wisdom and power of preaching in religious ecstatic trance.

The fourth linguistic confirmation that the word "stare" or "gaze" is used in an ASC context is that it appears as an aorist participle followed by a verb of seeing or saying in the aorist tense. This basic grammatical observation will probably "be Greek" to the majority of readers, but for scholars this grounds and supports the previous three markers. Taken together, Luke makes it clear that Stephen possesses the requisite ritual skills for inducing a religious trance.

4. The holy person requires tutelage by both a spirit and a real-life teacher. The adopting spirit familiarizes the holy person with the spirit world and its inhabitants, while a real-life teacher/holy person shares valuable personal experience in developing the life of holiness. Mark (1:13) indicates that while Jesus was in the desert angels ministered to him, which would include tutoring him, indeed preparing him for successful contest with an unclean spirit. John (3:22-23) explicitly states that Jesus became a disciple of John the Baptist after his own baptism and baptized others in the baptism of John. Along with John's other disciples, Jesus was tutored by him in pursuing a life of holiness pleasing to God.

We have no similar information concerning Stephen. However, given that he is the prime candidate put forward by the Hellenists as fulfilling the requisites of candidacy for ministry, it is reasonable to conclude that he had teachers and guides in the spirit world as well as in the community. These skills are not innate or self-taught.

5. The holy person becomes increasingly familiar with the adopting or possessing spirit. In the life of Jesus, the experience that tradition labels the "transfiguration" is an ASC experience of the spirit world by Jesus and select followers, each separately (Mark 9:2-10//Matt 17:1-9//Luke 9:28-36). Jesus has his experience, which isn't described; the evangelists tell us what the disciples saw. It is possible that Jesus was indeed speaking with the two identified figures (Moses and Elijah) from alternate reality. In any case, at the end of this event, Jesus feels assured that his mission, which has generated many powerful enemies, is indeed the one God has selected for him. The disciples in their turn are assured that this Jesus is indeed pleasing to God and worthy to be followed and supported: "this is my beloved Son; listen to him [more than to Moses and Elijah]" (Mark 9:7).

   As we noted earlier, the fact that Stephen immediately recognizes the beings he sees in the sky at the end of his speech suggests he has long-standing familiarity with them through previous similar experiences. This is certainly the testimony of generations of mystics.

6. The holy person continues to have religious trance (ASC) experiences after the initial revelation. Jesus tells his disciples that the father reveals things to him (Matt 11:25-27); he is certain that God hears him always (John 11:41-42). Indeed, Jesus communicates with God often (John 12:27-30). As noted earlier, ASCs are God's customary vehicles for communicating with human beings (1 Sam 3:1). We don't know Stephen's first and initiatory experience. But being quintessentially a man of his culture, Stephen not only

knows his renowned ancestors who themselves had ASC experiences (e.g., most recently, Jesus) but proves himself eminently personally capable of them too.

By grinding their teeth at him (Acts 7:54), the Sanhedrin signals its hostility and intent to harm him (Job 16:9; Ps 35:16; 37:12; 112:10; Lam 2:16). If he has not been in trance all along, Stephen slips into it now. It may have been induced or even deepened by his eloquent speech. Musicians and actors readily acknowledge that a good performance can induce trance on stage as well as in the audience. Indeed, if the performer can enter trance early in the performance, the entire experience will be richly dramatic for all. Stephen has a most vivid, rich, and rewarding vision experience just prior to his moment of death. He sees Jesus standing at the right hand of God. The British scholar J. Duncan M. Derrett noted that the standing Jesus is a broker or mediator, that is, someone presenting a case on behalf of a client. A seated Jesus, the more familiar New Testament image, is one who is exercising power. Therefore, seeing a standing Jesus assures Stephen that Jesus is interceding on his behalf with God, assuring his imminent welcome into the realm of God.

The Vision(s)

The final vision of Stephen is briefly reported:

> But he, full of the Holy Spirit, gazed into heaven and saw the glory of God, and Jesus standing at the right hand of God; and he said, "Behold, I see the heavens opened, and the Son of man standing at the right hand of God." (Acts 7:55-56)

Yet, brief as this report is (which means it is a very high-context report), it is possible to fill in many of the gaps with appropriate

cultural information. By describing Stephen as full of the Holy
Spirit, Luke reminds the reader that Stephen is a holy man. One
should interpret the subsequent information accordingly. A holy
man has ready access to the realm of God. That he can gaze into
the sky (literally, not heaven) and see the realm of God indicates
that he is definitely in Jerusalem. All of antiquity knew that
God's residence in the sky was directly over the earthy residence.
In the Israelite tradition the Jerusalem temple was God's earthly
residence, so God's location in the sky was directly above this.

In order to go from earth to the realm of God, one would have
to know where the entryway is, the "hole" in the sky. In the Israelite tradition, the hole is over Jerusalem. The Risen Jesus could
not have ascended to the sky in Galilee, since the hole was not
located there. Stephen, whom tradition says was killed in Jerusalem, perhaps most likely on Nablus Road some way from the
Damascus Gate, was looking in trance through the hole in the
sky into the realm of God. Stephen "gazed" into the sky (7:55)
and saw the hole, the opening (7:56).

What did he see there? First, the "glory of God" (7:55). In the
Israelite tradition, God's honor or glory, that is God's very self,
is manifested in light (Isa 60:1; 62:1; Luke 2:9). The light sometimes takes the form of a cloud (Exod 24:15ff) or fire (Deut 5:24)
flashing brightly (Ezek 1:4, 27-28; 10:4). Thus Stephen saw light,
or a bright color, which he interpreted, according to his tradition,
as the glory of God. South African anthropologists have identified three stages of trance. The first is to see colors or geometric
patterns. The sequence of colors seen in trance reflects neurologi-
cal changes. To see white is a sign of being in a trance. Orange
means the trance is weakening. Naturalistic colors indicate a
still weaker level of trance. To see actual distinct figures means
the trance is over. What is seen in trance is hazy and indistinct
(recall how often the risen Jesus was not recognized by those
who knew him in his earthly life). When one sees clearly, it is a
sign that the visionary has returned to the level of waking (so
called normal) consciousness.

That Stephen sees "the glory of God" indicates he is at the first stage of trance. The trance has begun, and he interprets the bright color as the glory of God. Then he sees Jesus standing at the right hand of God (7:55-56). He is now at the second stage of trance. In the second stage, the visionary strives to impose meaning on the colors or geometric patterns or other things she or he is seeing. That Stephen interprets this so clearly can mean one of two things. At a literary level, Luke has abbreviated and accelerated the process. At the level of trance itself, it can mean that Stephen is so habituated to the realm of God and its inhabitants that he can recognize them quickly.

Goodman identified four elements in a visionary's reactions to a trance experience. At first the visionary is 1) frightened and 2) doesn't recognize the person or object. 3) The person calms the visionary: "Fear not!" and 4) identifies himself or herself: "It is I." Once the visionary recognizes the person and is set at ease, the person communicates something of importance: a message from God, a new direction in life, a solution to a problem, and the like.[8] The fact that Stephen is not frightened by his vision but immediately recognizes the persons he is seeing confirms our judgment that Stephen is a holy man quite accustomed to trance experiences and to encounters with the realm of God and its inhabitants. There is no need for any self-identifications from God or from Jesus. Stephen understands the nonverbal communication of the scene perfectly.

Based on her fieldwork and research into religious ecstatic trance experiences, Dr. Felicitas D. Goodman identified four major kinds of ASCs that serve four human needs or desires: 1) healing, that is, the restoration of meaning to life (e.g., Acts 3:4); 2) divination, that is, seeking or learning the answer to a question or solution to a problem (e.g., Acts 16:9-10); 3) metamorphosis, the blurring of the boundaries between the human world and the realm of God in hopes of learning how to work change that is needed and/or desired among human beings (e.g., Acts 12:6-11); and 4) sky (or spirit) journeys, that is, visits to the realm of God similar to those reported by the astral prophets Ezekiel (e.g., Ezek 3:23-24) and John (e.g., Rev 4:1-2). As is evident in the Scripture citations noted in the parentheses of the previous sentence, the trance experiences reported in Acts fit into Dr. Goodman's categories. (Though not reported in Acts, Paul admits that he experienced a trip or sky journey to the realm of God in 2 Cor 12:1-5.)

How could we categorize Stephen's vision? It does provide him with meaning for his life, or at least confirms the meaning he believed his life and imminent death would have. Therefore, it could be a healing vision for him. But it could also be a divination vision, that is, it could be Stephen's attempt to "double-check" his judgment. He believed in and preached Jesus Messiah raised by God who made him Cosmic Lord. Stephen the Hellenist, along with other Hellenists, lived the Israelite traditions in a less strict way than the Hebrews. Concerns about the correctness of his views could have induced the trance that gave him a consoling answer. God was sufficiently pleased with Stephen to reveal the divine glory and presence to him, and Jesus was interceding on his behalf with God. This trance does not involve metamorphosis or a sky journey. Stephen will make that journey shortly after he dies. He will pass permanently from consensual reality into alternate reality.

In her early research, Dr. Goodman concluded "the trance experience itself is vacuous. If no belief system is proffered, it will remain vacuous. It is a neurophysiological event that receives content only from signals present in the respective culture."[9] Goodman's subsequent research further proved that neurophysiological events are not really vacuous, but always occur in the context of a belief system, a mythology, an ideology. Her ongoing research has confirmed that statement. Trance experiences thus are filled with culturally significant and expected scenarios. But without a key to interpret the experience, the visionary believes it to be vacuous. However, with the aid of a belief system, the visionary can interpret the visuals and provide the soundtrack and the interpretation. The understanding and interpretation of a vision derives from the culture, more specifically from what anthropologists call culture's latent discourse, or traditions of the culture, or "cultural dogma." A person learns and remembers these traditions, relying upon them for making sense out of experiences as needed.

In our scientific-minded culture, the latent discourse responds with skepticism to any mention of an ASC experience. Indeed, ASCs are often considered to be pathological or signs of pathology. In our culture, people who hear voices and communicate with persons who aren't there are said to be mentally ill. In contrast, for the biblical world the latent discourse was basically the Israelite tradition which believed that God's communication with human beings in ASC was normal. "Now the boy Samuel was ministering to the LORD under Eli. And the Word of the LORD was rare in those days; there was no frequent vision" (1 Sam 3:1). The prophets of Israel, as well as members of the Jesus movement and subsequent Jesus groups, all shared a common latent discourse. They interpreted their trance experiences within a framework that ASC experiences were normal. The dramatic change and reinterpretation of God's rules about clean and unclean foods (see Lev 11), which Peter learned in his trance reported in Acts 10, could only happen in an ASC experience of beings from the realm of God communicating to a human being. Only God could make that change since the rules were established by God in Leviticus.

For Stephen, the Hellenist view of the Israelite tradition served as his latent discourse. In this tradition, Stephen was a holy man even before being commissioned for ministry by the Twelve. He lived the tradition sincerely as a Hellenist, and he preached it with conviction. When faced with possible death for his convictions from fellow Israelites, Stephen boldly pleaded his case and joyously welcomed the unpleasant but not entirely unexpected outcome: a martyr's (that is, a witness's) death.

Conclusion

Stephen the holy man lived his Israelite traditions to the fullest within the framework of the Hellenistic interpretation of those traditions. He accepted the call to holiness and lived it intensely. This gave him intimate experience of the realm of God and its inhabitants. The brief information about the last phase of his life testifies that Stephen's entire life was lived in this fashion. Only in this way could he have died the way he did.

Though we have focused only on Stephen among the Seven, the only other minister in this group about whom Luke speaks explicitly and at length, Philip, is also portrayed as a holy man of similar stripe (Act 8:4-40). He was a successful preacher/evangelist (Acts 21:8), and he made a trance journey from the road to Gaza to Azotus (Acts 8:26-40). Moreover, he raised four daughters as holy women (Acts 21:9) who were unmarried prophetesses. Surely Philip was the real-life teacher of holiness for his daughters. Luke very likely would want the reader to conclude that these two, Stephen and Philip, are representative of the entire group.

CONCLUSION

Investigating in some depth Stephen and his companions as Hellenists, collectivists, ministers, and holy men, we have arrived at a better understanding of them. No doubt our new understanding differs considerably from the "popular" view, the understanding shared by the proverbial "person in the pew." While Benedict XVI shared similar fresh perspectives on Stephen with laypeople and others in his audience in January 2007, his insights might not yet have trickled down. Perhaps this short book will help.

However, we must take our reflections one step further. How do Stephen and his companions fit into Paul's social network? Since Paul witnessed and approved of Stephen's murder, how can Stephen be included in Paul's social network? To begin with, Paul, too, was a Hellenist. According to Luke in Acts, he was born and raised in a Hellenistic Israelite colony (to use Philo's term) in Tarsus (Asia Minor). His letters reveal a grasp of the Greek language and culture; he makes allusions to Greek literature. Still, his self-identification clearly indicates he was only minimally assimilated. In Philippians 3:5-6 he identifies himself thus: "circumcised on the eighth day, of the people of Israel, of the tribe of Benjamin, a Hebrew born of Hebrews; as to the law a Pharisee, as to zeal a persecutor of the church, as to righteousness under the law blameless." He was a Hellenist who strove to maintain his Israelite identity pure and unsullied. Witnessing Stephen's speech and death while simply minding the cloaks of those participating in the murder may have been decisive for turning Paul into a (more) active persecutor.

Paul's self-identification just cited also marks him as a collectivistic person. In the ancient world, persons identified themselves as a rule in terms of gender, genealogy, and geography. In Philippians Paul implies gender and geography (he's a male writing from one colony to another). But he is quite specific about his genealogy primarily in terms of kinship: an Israelite, a Benjaminite, members of a family practicing Hebrew customs devotedly. Notice that even though he can be identified as a Hellenist (at least by reason of language and culture), he insists on identifying himself as a "Hebrew born of Hebrews." A "Hebrew" at this time was a devout Israelite. Paul further identifies himself in terms of a fictive kinship affiliation, a surrogate family, namely: a Pharisee who was blameless regarding observance of the law.

This makes his part in the Stephen episode easy to understand. He disdains the Hellenists, he disagrees with fellow Hebrews (the Twelve) who empowered the Seven as ministers in their wrongheaded insistence that Jesus is Messiah. Thus far Stephen and Paul share two things in common: Hellenist and collectivistic identity. Yet, they view Hellenism differently with regard to Israelite traditions, and most certainly they disagree on Jesus-group beliefs and practices. And though both are collectivists, Paul would consider Stephen as part of an outgroup, most certainly not part of his elite Hebrew ingroup.

As everyone knows, something happened to Paul on his way to Damascus to persecute Jesus groups that dramatically changed his life. Following Luke's story line in Acts, it is quite plausible to propose a connection between Stephen's speech and Paul's experience. In his next appearance in Luke's story after Stephen's death, Paul is "still breathing threats and murder against the disciples of the Lord" (Acts 9:1). Something is obsessing Paul and consuming him. No doubt it was the Jesus groups with whom he was familiar in general. But it is also plausible that Paul, the Hellenist who shared colonial experience in common with Stephen, was mulling over Stephen's speech. While it enraged him, his continued reflection upon it undoubtedly made him reflect closely on what Stephen said. It preoccupied him and plausibly was affecting him subconsciously. The unconscious mind was making connections of which Paul was not yet aware.

On his journey to Damascus, Paul encounters the risen Jesus in an ASC experience that seemingly causes a sudden 180-degree turnaround in his life. However, was the change sudden, or had it already been set in motion by Stephen's speech? Paul's ASC experience testifies to the validity of his claim to be "blameless" in his observance of the law. In his own way, Paul is pleasing to God and favored by the deity with an encounter with the risen Jesus who is now in alternate reality. Paul the blameless Pharisee was a holy person. Even before accepting Jesus as Messiah, Paul believed God "set me apart before I was born, and had called me through his grace" (Gal 1:15-17). These phrases indicate that Paul viewed his birth as a prophetic calling. He was thus beloved of God ("called through his grace"), favored by God ("it pleased God"), and given the ascribed honor of the specific role of a prophet ("set me apart). Because his life was pleasing to God, it was possible for God to make contact with him in an ASC. What Paul was not prepared for, however, was the insight and instruction he would receive in this ASC.

As a result of this experience occasioned by Stephen's defense speech and death, Paul now fully embraced the Hellenist position. He preached to Hellenist Israelite minorities living among non-Israelite majorities. So incredible was it to his audiences, that Paul himself recorded their reactions: "'He who once persecuted us is now preaching the faith he once tried to destroy.' And they glorified God because of me" (Gal 1:23-24).

Was this a ministry? Was it similar to that of the Seven? This is an interesting part of Paul's story. Though Paul knew some of the Twelve personally, at least Peter and James the brother of the Lord (Gal 1:18), there is no indication that either of them commissioned him to ministry as the Twelve commissioned Stephen and his companions. Yet Paul insists that he is an apostle (Gal 1:1) commissioned by God himself (Gal 1:15-16). Is this a self-proclaimed ministry? Not if God determines it. Besides, the ministry to which God appointed Paul was that of prophet. In his letters Paul speaks of his *diakonia* (e.g., 2 Cor 6:3-4). Apparently, James, Peter, and John accepted it as well and by extending to Paul "the right hand of fellowship" called an end to hostilities between Hebrews and Hellenists on yet a second occasion (Gal 2:9).[1] Like the Hellenist Stephen, so too the Hellenist Paul was able to work out an agreement with the apostles and cement a place for himself in service to the believing community.

Stephen had an impact on Paul greater than he might ever have imagined. For this, his place in Paul's social network is quite legitimate and deserved.

NOTES

Introduction, pages ix–xxiii

1. "Non-Israelites" is my interpretation of "Gentiles," a word that for Israelites means peoples other than Israel. Paul went to regions where non-Israelites were in the majority, but his mission was to Israelite minorities living there. Many of those were Hellenists, as I will explain in the next chapter. The reasons behind such an interpretation are given at length in Bruce J. Malina and John J. Pilch, *Social Science Commentary on the Letters of Paul* (Minneapolis, MN: Fortress, 2006). See especially the Reading Scenarios: "Greeks and Israelites," 364–66; "Jew and Greek/Judean and Hellenist," 371–74. See also Bruce J. Malina and John J. Pilch, *Social Science Commentary on Acts of the Apostles* (Minneapolis, MN: Fortress, 2008).

2. Joseph A. Fitzmyer, *The Acts of the Apostles*, Anchor Bible 31 (Garden City, NY: Doubleday, 1998), 48–49.

3. Ekkehard W. and Wolfgang Stegemann, *The Jesus Movement: A Social History of Its First Century* (Minneapolis, MN: Fortress, 1999), 302.

4. Joseph Ratzinger/Pope Benedict XVI, *Jesus, The Apostles, and the Early Church* (San Francisco: Ignatius Press, 2007). His comments on Stephen were delivered at an audience on January 10, 2007, and can be read online: *http://www.ewtn.com/library/PAPALDOC/b16ChrstChrch27.htm*.

5. Malina and Pilch, *Social Science Commentary on the Letters of Paul*, 343–47.

6. Jerome Murphy-O'Connor, OP, *The Holy Land*, 2nd ed., rev. and exp. (Oxford: Oxford University Press, 1986), 125.

7. Lucian, *Epistola ad omnem ecclesiam, de revelatione corporis Stephani martyris*, trans. Avitus, in Migne, *Patrologia Latina* 41.807–818.

8. Murphy-O'Connor, *The Holy Land*, 93–94.

9. Elizabeth A. Clark, "Claims on the Bones of Saint Stephen: The Partisans of Melania and Eudocia," *Church History* 51 (1982): 141–156.

10. Kenneth G. Holum and Gary Vikan, "The Trier Ivory, 'Adventus' Ceremonial, and the Relics of St. Stephen," *Dumbarton Oaks Papers* 33 (1979): 127.

11. Jerome H. Neyrey, SJ, *The Passion According to Luke: A Redaction Study of Luke's Soteriology* (New York/Mahwah, NJ: Paulist Press, 1985), 69–107.

12. Dean P. Béchard, ed. and trans., *The Scripture Documents: An Anthology of Official Catholic Teachings* (Collegeville, MN: Liturgical Press, 2002).

13. See *http://www9.georgetown.edu/faculty/pilchj/CultJesus.htm.*

Chapter 1, pages 1–16

1. Arye Edrei and Doron Mendels, "A Split Jewish Diaspora: Its Dramatic Consequences," *Journal for the Study of the Pseudepigrapha* 16 (2007): 91–137.

2. Ibid., 91.

3. Leslie J. Hoppe, OFM, *The Synagogues and Churches of Ancient Palestine* (Collegeville, MN: Liturgical Press, 1994), 15–16.

4. Malina and Pilch, *Social Science Commentary on the Letters of Paul* , 337–39.

5. Heather A. McKay, "From Evidence to Edifice: Four Fallacies about the Sabbath," in *Text as Pretext: Essays in Honour of Robert Davidson,* ed. Robert P. Carroll, 179–99, JSOTSup 138 (Sheffield: JSOT Press, 1992); and Heather A. McKay, *Sabbath and Synagogue: The Question of Sabbath Worship in Ancient Judaism,* Religions in the Graeco-Roman World 122 (Leiden: E. J. Brill, 1994). Except for the archeological information drawn from Hoppe and Chiat, my conclusions about the synagogue are based on these two publications by McKay and an unpublished paper she presented at a seminar of the Society of Biblical Literature at which I was a copresenter.

6. Marilyn Joyce Segal Chiat, *Handbook of Synagogue Architecture,* Brown Judaic Studies 29 (Chico, CA: Scholars Press, 1981), 202.

7. Analysis of Stephen's speech is based mainly on Bruce J. Malina and John J. Pilch, *Social Science Commentary on Acts of the Apostles,* and Joseph A. Fitzmyer, SJ, *The Acts of the Apostles.*

Chapter 2, pages 17–35

1. Harry C. Triandis, *Individualism & Collectivism* (Boulder: Westview Press, 1995), 7. I have relied on his research to interpret the Bible since 1991 if not earlier. He has published extensively by himself and with coauthors. This work is foundational, and from a twenty-first century perspective somewhat prophetic when he looks into the future from his vantage point in 1995. As a tool for analyzing the past, this research is absolutely indispensable.

2. Bruce J. Malina, "The Social World Implied in the Letters of the Christian Bishop-Martyr (Named Ignatius of Antioch)," in *Society of Biblical Literature Seminar Papers*, vol. 2 (Missoula, MT: Scholars Press, 1978), 71–119. Though in this work Malina does not yet use the term "collectivist," he is describing that reality. At this point in his research he used the term "dyadic personality."

3. Bruce J. Malina, "The First-Century Personality: The Individual and the Group," in *The New Testament World: Insights from Cultural Anthropology*, 3rd ed., rev. and exp. (Louisville, KY: Westminster John Knox, 2001), 58–80; Bruce J. Malina and Jerome H. Neyrey, *Portraits of Paul: An Archaeology of Ancient Personality* (Louisville, KY: Westminster John Knox, 1996); John J. Pilch, *Introducing the Cultural Context of the Old Testament*, corr. and upd. ed. (Eugene, OR: Wipf & Stock, 2007a), 95–116; John J. Pilch, *Introducing the Cultural Context of the New Testament*. corr. and upd. ed. (Eugene, OR: Wipf & Stock, 2007b), 127–58.

4. Triandis, *Individualism & Collectivism*.

5. Geert Hofstede, "Empirical Models of Cultural Differences," in *Contemporary Issues in Cross-cultural Psychology*, eds. Nico Bleichrodt and Pieter J. D. Drenth, 4–20 (Amsterdam/Lisse and Berwyn, PA: Swets & Zeitlinger, 1991).

6. Pilch, *Introducing the Cultural Context of the Old Testament*, 97–98.

7. Pilch, *Introducing the Cultural Context of the New Testament*, 2007b, 130–33.

8. Triandis, *Individualism & Collectivism*.

9. Bruce J. Malina and Jerome H. Neyrey, *Portraits of Paul: An Archaeology of Ancient Personality*, 158–62.

10. This ongoing project of the British Academy is available in academic libraries but can also be investigated online: *http://www.lgpn.ox.ac.uk*. See also Margaret H. Williams, " The Use of Alternative Names by Diaspora Jews in Graeco-Roman Antiquity," *Journal for the Study of Judaism* 38 (2007): 307–27, who also agrees that Diaspora Israelites sometimes used alternative names to distinguish persons in the community with the same given name.

11. Williams, "The Use of Alternative Names," 323.

12. Bruce J. Malina and John J. Pilch, *Social Science Commentary on Acts of the Apostles*, see the comment on Acts 2:10.

13. Williams, "The Use of Alternative Names," 111–12 says this name is rarely found in Palestine; hence Stephanos is likely not a native of Palestine.

14. Ibid., 112 believes Philip was likely a Hellenized Israelite and not of colonial origin. At Acts 21:8 he is residing at Caesarea.

15. Ibid., 110 claims that a colonial origin is more plausible for Nicanor, since there are no contemporary Palestinian Nicanors. They are found mostly in Egypt and Cyrene.

16. Ibid., 111 hypothesizes that on the basis of the name and its "as" ending that he must have originally come from a Doric-speaking colony.

17. Richard Bauckham, *Jesus and the Eyewitnesses: The Gospels as Eyewitness Testimony* (Grand Rapids, MI and Cambridge, UK: Eerdmans, 2006).

18. Simon Hornblower, "Personal Names and the Study of the Ancient Greek Historians," in *Greek Personal Names: Their Value as Evidence*, eds. Simon Hornblower and Elaine Matthews, 129–143 (Oxford: Oxford University Press, 2000), 139.

19. Ibid., 142.

20. Ibid.

21. Scholars have recognized a pattern in history of naming the nameless in biblical materials. Bruce M. Metzger, "Names for the Nameless in the New Testament," in *Kyriakon: Festschrift Johannes Quasten in Two Volumes*, eds. Patrick Granfield and Josef A. Jungmann, 79–99 (Munster Westf: Aschendorff, 1970); John J. Pilch, "A Window into the Biblical World: The Samaritan Woman," *The Bible Today* 44, no. 4 (2006): 251–56; John J. Pilch, "A Window into the Biblical World: Naming the Nameless in the Bible," *The Bible Today* 44, no. 5 (2006): 315–20.

Chapter 3, pages 36–50

1. Frederick William Danker, ed. and rev., *A Greek-English Lexicon of the New Testament and other Early Christian Literature*, 3rd ed. (*BDAG*) (Chicago and London: University of Chicago Press, 2000).

2. Paul Bradshaw, ed., *The New Westminster Dictionary of Liturgy and Worship* (Louisville and London: Westminster John Knox, 2002).

3. The most current and critical study of *diakonia* was conducted by the Australian biblical scholar, John N. Collins, *Are all Christians Ministers?* (Collegeville, MN: Liturgical Press, 1992); and *Diakonia: Re-interpreting the*

Ancient Sources (New York and Oxford: Oxford University Press, 1990). This chapter is based on his research.

4. Collins, *Are all Christians Ministers?*

5. Malina and Pilch, *Social Science Commentary on the Letters of Paul.*

6. Collins, *Diaconia: Re-interpreting the Ancient Sources*, 230.

7. Ibid.

8. John J. Pilch, *Visions and Healing in the Acts of the Apostles: How the Early Believers Experienced God* (Collegeville, MN: Liturgical Press, 2004).

9. John J. Pilch, *Healing in the New Testament: Insights from Medical and Mediterranean Anthropology* (Minneapolis, MN: Fortress, 2000), 99, 105–6.

10. John J. Pilch and Bruce J. Malina, eds., *Handbook of Biblical Social Values* (Peabody, MA: Hendrickson Publishers, 1998), 72–75.

Chapter 4, pages 51–66

1. John J. Pilch, "Altered States of Consciousness in the Synoptics," in *The Social Setting of Jesus and the Gospels*, eds. Wolfgang Stegemann, Bruce J. Malina, and Gerd Theissen, 106–7 (Minneapolis, MN: Fortress, 2002).

2. Jean Clottes and David Lewis-Williams, *The Shamans of Prehistory: Trance and Magic in the Painted Caves*, text by Jean Clottes, trans. by Sophie Hawkes (New York: Harry N. Abrams, 1996), 14.

3. John J. Pilch, "Holy Men and their Sky Journeys," *Biblical Theology Bulletin* 35 (2005): 106–11.

4. John J. Pilch, *Visions and Healing in the Acts of the Apostles.*

5. John J. Pilch, "Altered States of Consciousness in the Synoptics," 107–8.

6. Bruce J. Malina and John J. Pilch, *Social Science Commentary on Acts of the Apostles.* See the reading scenarios "Holy Man"; and "ASC."

7. Ibid., and John J. Pilch, "Appearances of the Risen Jesus in Cultural Context: Experiences of Alternate Reality," *Biblical Theology Bulletin* 28 (1998): 52–60.

8. John J. Pilch, *Visions and Healing in the Acts of the Apostles*, 75.

9. Ibid., 4.

Conclusion, pages 67–70

1. Malina and Pilch, *Social Science Commentary on the Letters of Paul*, 195–96.

BIBLIOGRAPHY

Bauckham, Richard. *Jesus and the Eyewitnesses: The Gospels as Eyewitness Testimony*. Grand Rapids, MI and Cambridge, UK: Eerdmans, 2006.

Bradshaw, Paul, ed. *The New Westminster Dictionary of Liturgy and Worship*. Louisville, KY: Westminster John Knox, 2002.

Chiat, Marilyn Joyce Segal. *Handbook of Synagogue Architecture*. Brown Judaic Studies, 29. Chico, CA: Scholars Press, 1981.

Clark, Elizabeth A. "Claims on the Bones of Saint Stephen: The Partisans of Melania and Eudocia." *Church History* 51 (1982): 141–56.

Collins, John N. *Are all Christians Ministers?* Collegeville, MN: Liturgical Press, 1992.

———. *Diakonia: Re-interpreting the Ancient Sources*. New York and Oxford: Oxford University Press, 1990.

Cross, F. L., and E. A. Livingstone, eds. *Oxford Dictionary of the Christian Church*. 3rd ed. Revised. Oxford: Oxford University Press, 2005.

Danker, Frederick William, ed. and rev. *A Greek-English Lexicon of the New Testament and other Early Christian Literature*. 3rd ed. (*BDAG*). Chicago: University of Chicago Press, 2000.

Edrei, Arye, and Doron Mendels. "A Split Jewish Diaspora: Its Dramatic Consequences." *Journal for the Study of the Pseudepigrapha* 16 (2007): 91–137.

Fitzmyer, Joseph A., SJ. *The Acts of the Apostles*. Anchor Bible 31. Garden City, NY: Doubleday, 1998.

Hatzopooulos, Miltiades. "'L'histoire par les noms' in Macedonia." In Hornblower and Matthews, *Greek Personal Names*, 99–117.

Hofstede, Geert. *Culture's Consequences: International Differences in Work-Related Values*. Abridged edition. Beverly Hills, CA: Sage, 1984.

———. "Empirical Models of Cultural Differences." In Nico Bleichrodt and Pieter J. D. Drenth, eds. *Contemporary Issues in Cross-cultural Psychology*, 4–20. Amsterdam/Lisse and Berwyn, PA: Swets & Zeitlinger, 1991.

Holum, Kenneth G., and Gary Vikan. "The Trier Ivory, 'Adventus' Ceremonial, and the Relics of St. Stephen." *Dumbarton Oaks Papers* 33 (1979): 113, 115–33.

Hoppe, Leslie J., OFM. *The Synagogues and Churches of Ancient Palestine.* Collegeville, MN: Liturgical Press, 1994, 15–16.

Hornblower, Simon. "Personal Names and the Study of the Ancient Greek Historians." In Hornblower and Matthews, *Greek Personal Names,* 129–43.

Hornblower, Simon, and Elaine Matthews, eds. *Greek Personal Names: Their Value as Evidence.* Oxford: Oxford University Press for The British Academy, 2000.

Johnson, Luke Timothy. *The Acts of the Apostles.* Sacra Pagina 5. Collegeville, MN: Liturgical Press, 1991.

Malina, Bruce J. "The First-Century Personality: The Individual and the Group." In *The New Testament World: Insights from Cultural Anthropology.* Third edition revised and expanded, 58–80. Louisville, KY: Westminster John Knox, 2001.

———. "The Mediterranean Self: A Social Psychological Model." In *The Social World of Jesus and the Gospels.* New York and London: Routledge, 1996.

———. "The Social World Implied in the Letters of the Christian Bishop-Martyr (Named Ignatius of Antioch)." *Society of Biblical Literature Seminar Papers.* Vol. 2. Missoula, MT: Scholars Press, 1978, 71–119.

———. "Understanding New Testament Persons." In *The Social Sciences and New Testament Interpretation.* Peabody, MA: Henderson Publishers, 1996, 41–61.

Malina, Bruce J., and Jerome H. Neyrey, "First-Century Personality: Dyadic, not Individual." In *The Social World of Luke-Acts: Models for Interpretation.* Edited by Bruce J. Malina and Jerome H. Neyrey, 67–96. Peabody, MA: Hendrickson, 1991.

———. *Portraits of Paul: An Archaeology of Ancient Personality.* Louisville, KY: Westminster John Knox, 1996.

Malina, Bruce J., and John J. Pilch. *Social Science Commentary on Acts of the Apostles.* Minneapolis, MN: Fortress, 2008.

————. *Social Science Commentary on the Letters of Paul*. Minneapolis, MN: Fortress, 2006.

McKay, Heather A. "From Evidence to Edifice: Four Fallacies about the Sabbath." In *Text as Pretext: Essays in Honour of Robert Davidson*, edited by Robert P. Carroll, 179–99. JSOTSup, 138. Sheffield: JSOT Press, 1992.

————. *Sabbath and Synagogue: The Question of Sabbath Worship in Ancient Judaism*. Religions in the Graeco-Roman World, 122. Leiden: E. J. Brill, 1994.

Metzger, Bruce M. "Names for the Nameless in the New Testament." In *Kyriakon: Festschrift Johannes Quasten in Two Volumes*. Edited by Patrick Granfield and Josef A. Jungmann, 79–99. Munster Westf: Aschendorff, 1970.

Murphy-O'Connor, Jerome, OP. *The Holy Land*. 2nd ed., rev. and expanded (Oxford: Oxford University Press, 1986), 125.

Neyrey, Jerome, SJ. *The Passion According to Luke: A Redaction Study of Luke's Soteriology*. New York/Mahwah, NJ: Paulist Press, 1985.

Osiek, Carolyn. "Deacon." *New Interpreter's Dictionary of the Bible*. Vol. 2: D.H. Nashville: Abingdon, 2007.

Pilch, John J. "Altered States of Consciousness in the Synoptics." In *The Social Setting of Jesus and the Gospels*. Edited by Wolfgang Stegemann, Bruce J. Malina, and Gerd Theissen, 103–15. Minneapolis, MN: Fortress, 2002.

————. *Healing in the New Testament: Insights from Medical and Mediterranean Anthropology*. Minneapolis, MN: Fortress, 2000.

————. "Holy Men and their Sky Journeys." *Biblical Theology Bulletin* 35 (2005): 106–11.

————. *Introducing the Cultural Context of the Old Testament*. Corrected and updated edition. Eugene, OR: Wipf & Stock, 2007a.

————. *Introducing the Cultural Context of the New Testament*. Corrected and updated edition. Eugene, OR: Wipf & Stock, 2007b.

————. *Visions and Healing in the Acts of the Apostles: How the Early Believers Experienced God*. Collegeville, MN: Liturgical Press, 2004.

————. "A Window into the Biblical World: Naming the Nameless in the Bible." *The Bible Today* 44, no. 5 (2006): 315–20.

————. "A Window into the Biblical World: The Samaritan Woman." *The Bible Today* 44, no. 4 (2006): 251–56.

Pilch, John J., and Bruce J. Malina, eds. *Handbook of Biblical Social Values*. Peabody, MA: Hendrickson, 1998.

Schweizer, R. Eduard. "Ministry in the Early Church." *ABD* IV: 835–42.

Stegemann, Ekkehard W., and Wolfgang. *The Jesus Movement: A Social History of Its First Century.* Minneapolis, MN: Fortress, 1999.

Strelan, Rick. 2000. "Recognizing the Gods (Acts 14:8-10)." *NTS* 46 (2000): 488–503.

———. *Strange Acts: Studies in the Cultural World of the Acts of the Apostles.* (BZNW 126). Berlin/New York: De Gruyter, 2004.

Triandis, Harry C. *Individualism & Collectivism.* Boulder, CO: Westview Press, 1995.

Walter, Nikolaus, "Hellenistic Jews of the Diaspora at the Cradle of Primitive Christianity." In *The New Testament and Hellenistic Judaism.* Edited by Peder Borgen and Søren Giversen, 37–58. Peabody, MA: Hendrickson, 1997.

Williams, Margaret H. "Palestinian Jewish Personal Names in Acts." In *The Book of Acts in its First Century Setting.* Vol. 4: Palestinian Setting. Edited by Richard Bauckham, 79–113. Grand Rapids, MI: Eerdmans, and Carlisle: The Paternoster Press, 1995.

———. "The Use of Alternative Names by Diaspora Jews in Graeco-Roman Antiquity." *Journal for the Study of Judaism* 38 (2007): 307–27.

INDEX OF PERSONS AND SUBJECTS

Abibas, xv

Acts of the Apostles, ix, x, xi–xiii, xviii, xix, xxiii, 1, 2, 5, 12, 15, 27, 36, 37, 41, 43, 46, 47, 53, 55, 58, 64, 67, 68

Alexander the Great, 2, 3, 32

allocentrism, 19

Altered State of Consciousness (ASC), x, 48, 53, 54, 55, 57, 60, 65, 69; kinds of, 63

ancient synagogues, 7–8, 9

Antiochus Epiphanes IV, 2

apocrypha/apocryphal books, 4–6

Aramaic language, x, 1, 3, 5, 6, 22, 45

awareness, levels of, xxiii, 48, 53

Barnabas, x

Bauckham, R., 33

Benedict XVI, xii, xiii, xxii, xxiii, 36, 67

Bible, in different language, 1, 3, 5–6

bone relics, xv–xvii

circumcision, 7

collective societies, xii, xxii

collectivism, 17

collectivists, 17, 18–28, 29, 30, 68

Collins, J. N., 37, 43, 44, 45, 46–47

companions, xii, xxii, xxiii, 5, 15, 36, 51, 52–55, 56, 67, 69

Context Group, xx

Cyrenians, 10

Danker, F., 37

deacons, xii, xxii, 39

deacons, origin of, 37

deacons, permanent, 36

Decree on the Apostolate of the Laity, 47

Derrett, J. D. M., 61

diakonia, 38, 40–46, 47, 48, 70

Diakonos, 37–40, 43

Diasporas, 4–6

Diocletian, xv

École Biblique et Archéologique Française, xvi

Edrei, A., 4

Epiphanius of Salamis, ix

Ethea, xv

Eudocia, xvi, xvii

Gamaliel, xiv–xv

Gentiles, xi

Goodman, F. D., 63–64

Gordon's Tomb," xiii

ḥasid, 52, 57
healing, 48, 50, 55, 57, 63, 64
Hebrews, 1, 2, 5, 12, 13, 21, 22,
    23, 27, 30, 34, 39, 44, 52, 64, 68,
    70
Hellenists, ix, x, xii, xxii, 1, 2, 5,
    7, 10, 14, 15, 21–23, 27, 30, 44,
    48, 51, 52, 67, 68, 70
Holiness Code, 51
holy person, 48, 52–55; call to be,
    56–61
Hornblower, S., 33, 34
humanities, xx

idiocentrism, 19
Ignatius of Antioch, on deacons,
    39
individualistic societies, xii
individualists, xii, 18–28, 30
ingroups, 21–22
*Interpretation of the Bible in the
    Church*, xx

Jesus, on trial, xviii, xix
Judeans, x, xi, xii, 4, 16, 27, 32

*Lexicon of Greek Personal Names
    (LGPN)*, 30, 31, 33, 34
Lucian, xiv, xv
Luke the evangelist, xi, xix; as
    author of Acts, xi, xx, xxii,
    xxiii, 15, 30, 41, 43, 49, 57, 67
Lumen Gentium, 36, 56

Malina, B., 17, 57
McKay, H., 8, 9
Mendels, D., 4

ministry, 27, 28, 42, 43, 46, 47, 49,
    60, 69
Mishnah, xiii
Murphy-O'Connor, J., xiii

Neyrey, J., xviii–xx
Nicodemus, xiv, xv, 29

oral tradition, 6
outgroups, 22

Paul, vii, ix, x, xix, 1, 2, 30, 31, 38,
    43; as Hellenist, xi, 15, 67, 68,
    70; an ASC experience, 55, 64,
    69
Paul VI, Pope, 36
Pilch, J., 28, 52, 56, 57
Pontifical Biblical Commission,
    xx
proselyte, 31–32
Ptolemy, 3
Pulcheria, xvii

Sabbath observance, 8, 56; wor-
    ship, 8, 9
ṣaddiq, 52, 57
Sanhedrin, ix, xii, xiv, xviii, xix,
    15, 58, 61
Selimus, xv
Septuagint, 1, 3–4, 5, 6, 10, 15, 23,
    31, 37, 48
Seven, the, xx, xxii, 34, 37, 41, 49,
    51, 66, 68; names of, 28–33
social patterns, comparison of,
    24–28
Stegemann, E. W., xi, xii
Stephen, x; death of, ix, x, xiii;
    burial, xiv; speech, 10–15; as a
    collectivist, 21–24; meaning of

name, 32; first deacon, 41; and
  ministry, 49–50; a holy man,
  51–52, 62, 65; in a trance, 59,
  63; as Hellenist, 67, 68
synagogue of the Freedmen, 7, 9,
  10, 23
synagogues, x, 6, 7–10, 58

Targumim, 3, 6
tent of witness, 13, 14
Theodosius, xvi, xvii
Theodotus, 5, 8, 9
Torah, 3, 5, 7

Townsend, J., 52
trance, 53, 55, 57, 58, 59, 60, 61,
  62, 63, 64, 65, 66
Trial of Jesus, xviii, xix
Triandis, H., 17, 28
Twelve, the, xxii, 1, 23, 27, 28, 30,
  38, 39, 44, 45, 46, 47, 48, 49, 50,
  51, 65, 69

visionary's reaction to trance, 53,
  63, 64
visions, of Stephen, 61–66

Williams, M. H., 31

SCRIPTURE INDEX

Gen

23:15	28
23:16-20	12
24	xxi
24:24	28
24:31-32	xxi
24:33	xxi
24:49	xxi
24:52	xxi
24:54	xxi
33:19	12

Exod

4:10	12
7:3	49
15:26	46
20:8-11	8
24:15ff	62

Lev

11	65
17–26	51
19:2	51, 56

Deut

4:34	49
5:24	62
6:18	46
12:25	46
13:18	46

17:7	xiv
23:2	11
28:46	49
29:2	49
34:11	49

Josh

24:32	12

1 Sam

3:1	xiii, 48, 57, 60, 65

2 Kgs

17:6	4

Isa

8:18	49
57:3	11
60:1	62
60:17	39
62:1	62

Jer

30:2	55
36:2, 28	55

Ezek

1:4, 27-28	62
3:23-24	64

10:4	62	*Ezra*	
14:7	32	4:1-3	34
Hos		*Sir*	
1:2	11	30:1	11
Amos		*Wis*	6
5:25-27	13	3:1-9	5
		18:4	5
Hab		*Matt*	
2:2	55	11:25-27	60
		11:27	11
Pss		16:17	28
35:16	61	17:1-9	60
37:12	61	20:26-28	38
112:10	61	20:28	41
135:9	49		
		Mark	
Job		1:13	59
16:9	61	1:24	52
		3:31-35	29
Prov		5:41	6
10:4	37	7:3-5	6
		7:9-13	6
Eccl		9:2-10	60
1:9	14	9:35	38
		10:35-45	29
Lam		10:46	28
2:16	61	14:56	xviii
Esth		*Luke*	
1:10	37	1:5	29
2:2	37	2:9	62
6:3, 5	37	4:20	57
		5:10	28
1 Macc	6, 32	4:39	48
		6:7, 11	Xix
2 Macc	6, 32	6:22-23	xix
		7:31-35	xix
4 Macc	32	7:36	29
9:17	38		

7:40	29	1:10	57
8:3	28	1:15	43
9:46	29	1:15, 17, 25	43
10:1	Ix	1:17, 25	41, 43
10:13-16	xix	1:17, 26	46
11:37	29	1:21-22	23, 43
11:47-51	xix	1:23	43
12:8-12	xix	1:24	43
12:11-12	xix	1:26	43
13:33-34	xix	2:7	45
18:10	29	2:10	31, 32
19:14, 17	xix	2:36	21
20:1-7	xviii	2:42	xxiii
20:10-15	xix	2:43	49
21:12-15	xix, 58	2:44-47	45
21:14-15	xix	2:46	22
21:15	xix	3:1	22
22:43	48	3:1-10	48
22:54	xviii	3:4	55, 57, 63
22:56	57	3:4, 12	57
22:66-71	xviii	4:30	49
22:69	xviii	4:32	30
23:1-5, 6-12	xviii	4:32-35	45
23:13-25	xviii	4:35	45
23:32, 34, 39-43	xviii	4:36	29
23:46	xviii	5:12	49
		5:19-21	22
John		5:42	22, 47
1:46	29	6	21, 37, 44,
3	xiv		45, 46, 47
3:1	29	6:1	39
3:22-23	59	6:1-6	21, 40
4:9	29	6:1–7:1	10
11:41-42	60	6:1–8:3	ix
12:27-30	60	6:2	xviii, 30, 44,
19:20	5		45, 46
		6:3	23, 46
Acts		6:4	39, 42, 46
1:8	43	6:5	30, 49

6:5, 7	56
6:8	49, 53, 57
6:9	xviii, xix, 7, 10, 23
6:10	xix, 50, 59
6:11	11
6:11-14	xix
6:12	xix
6:12-15	xviii
6:13	11
6:13-14	xviii, 11, 15
6:14	11, 15
6:15	57, 58, 59
6:38	11
6:44-50	11
6–7	xix
7:2	11
7:2-53	11, 49, 50, 59
7:7	12
7:8	49
7:20	15
7:22	12
7:35	12
7:36	49
7:37	13
7:39-43	13
7:39-50	13
7:44-50	13
7:51	11
7:51-53	xix
7:52-53	12
7:53-54	53
7:54	11, 42, 61
7:55	55, 56, 57, 62
7:55-56	48, 57, 61, 63
7:56, 58, 59, 60	xviii
8:1, 4	xviii
8:2	xiv
8:4-40	66
8:9-13, 18-24	48, 54
8:26-40	66
9:1	68
9:15	43
10	65
10:4	55, 57
11:6	55, 57
11:19	x, 23, 49
11:19-20	23
11:20	10, 23
11:29	42
12:6-11	63
12:25	42
13:9	30, 57
13:16-43	31
13:43	32
14:3	49
14:9	55, 57
15	7
15:12	49
19:9-10	63
18:2	29
19:22	41
20:24	43
20:25	41
21:19	42, 44
21:8	30, 66
21:9	66
21–24	xix
22:17	x
22:20	xi
22:21	xi
22:3	xiv
23:1	57
25–26	xix

Rom		2:9	70
3:9	ix, 1, 2	6:10	29
11:13	41		
15:31	42	*Phil*	
16:1	38, 39	1:1	38, 39
		1:15-16	69
1 Cor		3:5	29
1:22-24	ix, 1, 2	3:5-6	15, 67
7:18	7		
10:32	1	*1 Thess*	
12:13	1	3:2	38
2 Cor		*1 Tim*	
3:7, 13	57	3:1-13	39
3:16, 18	42	3:8	39
5:18	41, 42		
6:3	42	*Titus*	
6:3-4	38, 70	1:12	29
8:4	42		
9:1	42	*Phlm*	
9:13	42	13	41
12:1-5	64		
		Rev	
Gal		1:10	54
1:1	69	4:1-2	64
1:15-17	69	4:2	54
1:18	69	17:3	54
1:23-24	69	21:20	54